T0168223

Wo... ...isdom
The Library of Perennial Philosophy

The Library of Perennial Philosophy is dedicated to the exposition of the timeless Truth underlying the diverse religions. This Truth, often referred to as the *Sophia Perennis*— or Perennial Wisdom—finds its expression in the revealed Scriptures as well as the writings of the great sages and the artistic creations of the traditional worlds.

Death as Gateway to Eternity: Nature's Hidden Message appears as one of our selections in the Perennial Philosophy series.

The Perennial Philosophy Series

In the beginning of the twentieth century, a school of thought arose which has focused on the enunciation and explanation of the Perennial Philosophy. Deeply rooted in the sense of the sacred, the writings of its leading exponents establish an indispensable foundation for understanding the timeless Truth and spiritual practices which live in the heart of all religions. Some of these titles are companion volumes to the Treasures of the World's Religions series, which allows a comparison of the writings of the great sages of the past with the perennialist authors of our time.

Cover:
The Blue Mountains,
Ténéré (Sahara) desert, Niger

DEATH AS GATEWAY TO ETERNITY
Nature's Hidden Message

by

Hans Küry

Translated by
Gillian Harris

Death as Gateway to Eternity:
Nature's Hidden Message
© 2013 World Wisdom, Inc.

Translated by Gillian Harris

Library of Congress Cataloging-in-Publication Data

Küry, Hans.
    [Wissende Tod. English]
    Death as gateway to eternity : nature's hidden message /
by Hans Küry ; translated by Gillian Harris.
        pages cm. -- (The perennial philosophy series)
    Includes bibliographical references and index.
    ISBN 978-1-936597-21-5 (pbk. : alk. paper) 1. Future life.
I. Title.
    BL535.K8713 2013
    202'.3--dc23
                                                    2012047742

Printed on acid-free paper in the United States of America

For information address World Wisdom, Inc.
P.O. Box 2682, Bloomington, Indiana 47402-2682
www.worldwisdom.com

CONTENTS

PREFACE

What is the meaning of the word "meditation," which recurs in the chapter headings of this book? I would answer thus: most books seek conversation with their readers. In contrast, meditation, in the strict sense, is a conversation of the author with himself; a discussion, if you will, with his own inner self, with his heart, with his innermost secret. Thus, to promulgate a secret means to reveal something of himself. When someone has meditations published, he does it for the sake of those fellow wayfarers who, like himself, are "underway" to discovering the meaning of life and the meaning of the world. One man's self-communion can also be to others' benefit.

It is no coincidence that the word "way" has just occurred twice. There is a close connection between the words "sense" (or "meaning") and "way." The linguists tell us that in early times the German word *Sinn* meant "direction," but also "way." *Sich besinnen* (to meditate) could therefore mean "to seek the right way." One thinks spontaneously of Tao, which—as the scholars teach us—stands in Chinese for "way" or "path" and for "meaning." In a certain sense all living beings, indeed all created things, are underway: man, too, is underway. And he alone among all creatures seeks to find out whence his way comes and whither it leads.

It seems to me that this essential relationship between "way" and "meaning" is connected with the fact that most typical seekers of meaning, most philosophical minds, have a predilection for walking, for pacing to and fro, for strolling and rambling. Aristotle's disciples, who philosophized as they strolled in great halls, were no isolated case. And in many places one finds "philosophers' paths," designated as such or not, remote, quiet trails where one may hold conversations undisturbed. In my youth I, too, exchanged ideas with my contemporaries in such a place. At that time I also adopted the habit of jotting down unexpected insights—"flashes of inspiration"—on loose pieces of paper or in little notebooks, in short rest breaks or even while walking, before they vanished from my memory, never to be seen again.

In this kind of writing my own ideas were interwoven with images and metaphors of God's world around me, with the skies and clouds, trees and grasses, birds and stars.

Such a dialogue of man with the natural world in which he is nestled, flourishes perhaps most luxuriantly in the mountains, whose peaks are both near to Heaven and high above the populated valley floors. The Eternal wafts around the walker—not necessarily the ambitious mountaineer, but rather the tranquil stroller—at every step. Many questions urgent and constricting in the breast suddenly find the liberating answer.

One speaks of excursions,[1] and indeed! The wonderful walks I once took during a sojourn in the mountains with my dear wife—how long ago it seems, and yet in truth how recent!—were like an eagle's beatifying flight. The notebooks I had with me were filled, but my thoughts circled increasingly and involuntarily around the phenomenon of death. It appeared more as a Yes than a No. My wife was the first to read the collected observations, as they are presented here. She died unexpectedly shortly afterward. Had the mountains foreseen this turn of events and answered my anxious questions from the outset?

H.K.

1 In German, *Ausflüge*, literally "flights out." —Translator

First Meditation

◇ ◇ ◇

Of Judgment

1

External Causes of Doubt Concerning Life after Death, and the Belief in It

If many Westerners today find it difficult to believe in the immortality of the soul, the main reason lies in their living consciously only in quite superficial layers of human nature, in those layers which are indeed impermanent. They are consumed by the factual reality of their profession, their family, their outer destiny; but since all these facts are constantly changing throughout life, it would be more than audacious to believe in their continued existence after the profound caesura of death. Name, title, rank in society, in the church, in the state, possession of money, talent, expertise, reputation: in short, everything on which the consciousness of self of so many people is based—how are we to salvage all this beyond the grave?

It is a different matter for the man who believes, prays, and concentrates on God; the vibrations of higher, celestial states touch him from within. Although these states are sometimes difficult to grasp, they nonetheless have the effect, already in this earthly existence, of making the above-mentioned external facts pale by comparison: at best these still have meaning in their connections with inner realities, as symbols of something abiding, something immutable, that lies behind them.

Insofar as some wealthy businessman feels himself to be a businessman, with all the trappings of a privileged existence in society, he vanishes when he dies; if he does not see more deeply, he can scarcely believe in the immortality of his soul. If, however, he feels independent of the role he plays on earth, as a "poor soul" (a soul divested of all the wealth of transitory realities), then, even while still in the current of the impermanent, it is easier for him to see, or perhaps only to guess at, something permanent and immortal within himself.

Let us turn to the traditional hunting, shepherding, or farming peoples, e.g., the Native Americans or the Bedouins: their simple way of life, restricted to the bare necessities, already helps them to sever themselves more easily from external contingencies than is possible for the agitated members of a modern city culture, exposed to a thousand enticements.

Into what depths of his own soul does a Native American visionary plunge, as he sojourns for days, indeed weeks, upon a mountain in solitary contemplation? What lofty inner wealth—lying above all contingency—is surveyed by the mind of a Shaykh who for days does nothing but invoke the Name of

God, surrounded on all sides by the vast monotony of the desert?

From the point of view of the average Westerner of today, one can no sooner resolve the question of immortality than one could seek the constellations in the night sky from a harshly-lit urban street; the artificiality of present-day life and the satanic clamor of current events in the press, radio, and television drown out the inner truths of the soul as insolently as the glare of electric lights effaces the shining of the stars.

But if we betake ourselves to those sages of the traditional peoples, it is as if we were to step out of the city, glittering with a thousand illusions, into the lonely black night, and suddenly see the starry heavens above us with perfect clarity. The prophets and saints of all peoples have affirmed the immortality of the human soul. Did they not indeed have deeper insight than the fast-moving man of today, who because of the sheer volume of impressions tumbling one upon the next, no longer comes to reflection, let alone meditation, upon the Immutable?

The man plunged in God sees the paradisal and infernal states not as lying in the future, entering into play only after death; he sees them already now, in earthly life, rather as we can hear the corresponding chord upon a tone in our auditory imagination, even if that chord is not actually sounding.

In any case the "posthumous" states cannot be categorized in "temporal" terms. If, as is repeatedly testified, the dying man sees his whole life pass before him again, this overview indicates that he is entering simultaneity or non-temporality.

2

Concerning Man's Situation on Earth

The key to man's destiny after death lies hidden in his existence here below. There is unanimous agreement that the states which the soul must traverse after death are consequences of its knowledge or its errors in the here-below. Thus all observations concerning the immortality of the soul are linked with the question of the nature and vocation of man.

Even the most fleeting comparison of man with the myriads of beings populating the earth besides him, teaches him to recognize in himself a culmination, an exception, a creature illumined by the Spirit. He is, as the book of Exodus says, the image of God.

Of course more ingenuity and also more wisdom is given to animals—indeed to plants, and even rocks!—than the average nature-alienated man of today would care to admit. Besides, it is certainly not the case that man outstrips his fellow beings in everything; on the contrary, every plant and animal species and every kind of mineral is unrivaled in one or other of its attributes. Seen from the standpoint of the divine Creation, all beings, from crystal to man, are wondrous works, of which each manifests an aspect of the divine Reality and none can be understood in its profoundest depths by man, otherwise he would necessarily have the capacity to recreate it. And does not man remain a secret even unto himself, a creation out of whose smallest cell speaks God's unfathomable wisdom, beside which our human wisdom is a sheer nothingness?

All creatures are as it were God-spoken words, whose profundity no man can plumb. In terms of this image, man, among all the many words, could be equated with the word of God. In a certain sense all creatures are equally profound and equally significant, just as all words, whether they designate elevated or lowly things, manifest the mystery of the word in equal manner, i.e., the descent of a spiritual meaning into a purely physical series of sounds. In another sense, however, man is pre-eminent in the family of earthly creatures, just as the word "God" surpasses all other words. As such, it, too, is a word like the others: however, by virtue of what it designates, it is superior. Man, too, is on one hand a creature like all others (woe betide him if he forgets this side of his being and proclaims himself the "supreme being"!); on the other hand, however, man is the image of God and thereby superior to the other creatures.

The superiority of man on earth as an image of God is manifested *outwardly* by his *centrality*. Just as the hub of a wheel contains the point of attachment of all the spokes that radiate outwards, so, too, man bears *in potentia* within himself the sum of all possibilities that are unfolded in the animals, plants and minerals. Thus Adam had the capacity to give all of them their true names, and that meant something entirely different from giving them scientific names according to some external characteristic; it meant seeing them in their innermost condition as words of God and finding an exact correspondence in the primordial human language. For the man close to God, the animals, plants, and minerals are more than mere metaphors for individual attributes, as assigned to them by the tellers of fables. The lion, for example, is not only the model of courage: its mane, resembling an aureole, its yellow hue, its roaring voice, and also the depth of its gaze and the completeness in its movements and behavior, elevate it to the rank of a solar animal and a symbol of the divine Majesty.

3

Of the Divine Word

Outwardly, vis-à-vis the world's creatures, man's mission as priest and image of God is manifested by his centrality. But *inwardly, in the domain of man himself*, it is manifested by the fact that God has spoken directly with him in his own language.

Of course it is ultimately incorrect to say that God has spoken to man in human language; for human language has a secret dimension of depth, and it is God's language by virtue of this.

It is curious how indifferent people are today to the phenomenon of language. A tool for the expression of ideas, which originated in antiquity, when living conditions were very simple, and still serves today, under completely different conditions, ramified in a million ways; a means of understanding, in which the most adverse minds and the most antagonistic temperaments can converse; a conceptual net whose interstices are narrow enough to hold fast the essential, but at the same time wide enough to filter out what is too particular, what confuses understanding; a world of sounds with which the poets can evoke feelings, ideas, and experiences in us: has any man ever been in a position to invent so splendid a creation, or could it—half by chance, half on purpose—have evolved from the clumsy cry of an animal? (The word "evolve" has gradually become a maid-of-all-work to explain the unexplainable!)

But language has another, quite different side, a side that is not addressed in textbooks: words, according to who speaks them, who is listening, and in what situation they are spoken, can have a completely different content: the simplest word, spoken at the right *moment* and in the right circumstances, can become an event of unimaginable scope. The divine Word has the greatest scope. In the formidably right choice of moment—recalling the hour of Judgment— the above-mentioned "divine dimension of depth in language" reveals to us that God Himself is speaking. Apparently simple words spoken in divine hours become bearers of revelations of the hereafter. For example, the two words of Christ with which he chose his disciples—"Follow me!"—are weightier than a whole library of theological erudition. Or one may recall the seven words or sayings spoken by Christ on the cross, each of which has become a guiding star for man in the night of this world.[1]

Why is the Word of God inimitable? Why have even the poets been unable to write a fifth Gospel or compose new psalms? Why has no Arab poet attempted to add a *surah* to the Koran, and why has no Hindu ever succeeded in providing a sequel to the books of the Veda? The Word of God is inimitable because it is spoken in human and divine language simultaneously: because apart from human thought it incorporates the "divine Instant" if one may express it thus. The human side may be imitated, but the divine may not.

The "divine Instant" (the German mystics spoke of the *Nu*) is Now. Whereas past and future are subject to time, the Now is time-less. (As soon as we believe we have laid hold upon the Now, it is already no longer

---

1 The seven last words or sayings of Christ are: "Father, forgive them; for they know not what they do" (Luke 23:34); "Verily I say unto thee, Today shalt thou be with me in paradise" (Luke 23:43); "Woman, behold thy son! . . . Behold thy mother!" (John 19:26-27); "My God, My God, why hast thou forsaken me?" (Matthew 27:46 and Mark 15:34); "I thirst" (John 19:28); "It is finished" (John 19:30); and "Father, into thy hands I commend my spirit" (Luke 23:46).

the Now, but the past, even by a mere fraction of a second.) The Now of the divine Word is reflected for us human beings in a certain "historical" moment, in an hour of Judgment, in a fateful point in time. However, seen from *within*, the Now of the divine Word is timeless and eternal. "Heaven and earth will pass away, but my words will not pass away" (Matthew 24:35).

4

Tradition and the Immortality of the Soul

Man, to whom the divine Word is addressed, must also be absorbed in the eternity of the divine Now, the divine Word, the divine Instant (*Nu*). The divine Word is only Reality when man, to whom it is addressed, hears it. But if the divine Word is eternal, the hearing of it, which gives it its reality, must also be eternal:

> Verily, verily I say unto you: He that heareth my word and believeth on him that sent me, hath everlasting life and shall not come into condemnation; but is passed from death unto life. (John 5:24)

Hearing the divine Word, man is given the possibility to pass from impermanence into permanence; the divine Word is as it were the sacred drum, whose vibrations are sown into the hearing being and recall all layers to consciousness, right to the innermost. Thanks to the divine Word, man, if he is able to grasp it, has the possibility opened to him of remaining posthumously in a prolongation of the human state, in a certain sense. This possibility is the crown of the human state, its fulfillment and its deepest meaning.

Thus the only human act that is meaningful and ultimately worth the effort is listening to the divine Word. But included in listening to the divine word is the exact transmission of what God has said to humanity or sectors of humanity. The great religions of humanity have been given the colorless name "traditions," and rightly so, for what matters principally for man is transmitting the word of God with utmost precision, excluding all human admixture. It is a calamity of the greatest order when men begin to measure the Word of God according to their own understanding, and force it into the framework of human conceptualization, or even cast it aside and mock it: in this way one cheats oneself and others of salvation.

5

Divine Word and Judgment

The eternity of damnation[2] is based upon the fact that all those addressed by the divine Word are included in its eternity, even if they refuse to hear it. Of course, they are situated not in the Now but on a lower level of eternity, which one could designate as the Forever. The medieval sages were already differentiating between the levels of eternity. The lower levels of eternity or non-temporality could perhaps be called simultaneity: what unfolds in time as a sequence is immediately present, like a powerful chord. From the viewpoint of Judgment, "simultaneity" means on

---

2 Some readers may take offence at our measuring the fate of men in the hereafter by the hard and rigorous yardstick of the great religions. Is there no divine Mercy, then? Certainly; and precisely since we believe unconditionally in God's mercy, we differentiate sharply between what is God's and what is man's. The more ruthless man is in judging himself—not his neighbor!—the greater the Grace allotted to him by Heaven. To forgive oneself everything indiscriminately impedes God to a certain degree, one could almost say, from exercising clemency from His side. To a certain degree: for one day everything will return to God, whence it originated (teaching of the Apocalypse, the return of all things). It is just that this vision infinitely surpasses man!

one hand that the paradisal response, i.e., beatitude, shines instantly upon the soul in good works (from meditation and prayer to spiritual sacrifice), and on the other hand, that the infernal response becomes instantly visible to the soul in sin (from conceptual error to hardening of the heart and misdeeds). Souls in which the good was preponderant enjoy Paradise as a "reward," i.e., a state of peace with themselves, but souls in which evil had the upper hand suffer hell as a punishment, i.e., a state of conflict with themselves; according to all revelations the consciousness of merit or guilt belongs to Paradise and hell respectively.

In contrast, the higher level of eternity or non-temporality would be the timelessness of the Now, i.e., unconditional freedom from the law of time, from the disintegration of unity, be it disintegration into a sequence, a succession, or into a simultaneity, an adjacency of opposing poles. If man's right eye symbolizes the past, his left eye symbolizes the future: the Now, not manifested outwardly—because it would burn everything to ashes—is the third eye, the eye of Shiva, the eye on the forehead above the base of the nose (*ajna chakra*) upon which spiritual concentration is directed. Earth, hell, and heaven are swallowed up in the Now, in the Instant (*Nu*); thus it is said that those who have practiced concentration in life will sit directly beneath the throne of the world

DEATH AS GATEWAY TO ETERNITY: NATURE'S HIDDEN MESSAGE

Judge, hidden and protected. In earliest childhood the soul thinks neither of yesterday nor tomorrow, it lives in the present and close to the Now, which shines upon it like a sun, bright and warm. The happiness of a child is thus a glimmer of beatitude, and perhaps, in the case of saints, even a glimmer of the Now.

The nearness of the child to the heavenly Center is also reflected in his appearance: compared to that of an adult, his head is more spherical, thus in closer correlation with the Center; it represents so to speak an orb in miniature. A child's limbs are incomparably more pliant than those of an old person; this high degree of mobility corresponds to the great wealth of possibilities in the realm of the Center. Finally, we may remember the child's gift, in spirit and soul, of rapidly acquiring one or even several languages through imitation and intuition: since he is near to the heavenly Center, he is also near to the paradisal primordial language, from which all individual human languages have sprung; the great difficulty a man has in learning a foreign language in his later years shows how far he has distanced himself from that central state.

And it is no less indicative that—in normal circumstances—food, clothing, and other necessities are bestowed upon a child without effort on his part; it is as if he is still in Paradise, and, unlike the "fallen" man, does not need to earn his bread "by the sweat of his brow."

6

Time and Judgment

Like the Word of God, the Last Judgment is an eruption of the Now, the divine Instant (*Nu*), into time. The soul of the deceased is judged—or rather, it judges itself—when it makes the transition from the temporal domain to the non-temporal. As long as the soul is situated within the temporal domain, it has free choice, it still has "time" to decide thus or thus, for or against God; but when it has made the transition into the non-temporal domain its choice is definitive: *"time" has run out*, it will never again have time to revoke its choice, and this final choice, taken by the soul itself, is Judgment.

When time, or at least a temporal cycle, ends, all men living in this temporal domain necessarily reach the domain of the *non-temporal*; this is the Last Judgment in the sense of "the end of time." What men have chosen in this decisive moment, they have chosen forever: they are judged.

From the viewpoint of non-temporality, the interval between individual judgment and the Last Judgment disappears, precisely because from this standpoint time is no more.

Thus it is only an apparent contradiction when in the religions it is sometimes said that the soul is judged immediately after death, and sometimes, that it will be brought to reckoning only on the Day of Judgment; this supposed contradiction is explained by the difficulty for human thought of grasping conditions lying beyond time. A similar apparent contradiction is produced when one considers various lesser and greater temporal ages or cycles; from the purely temporal point of view lesser and greater judgments follow one another as conclusions of this age, but seen non-temporally or supra-temporally, there can be no interval between the different judgments; thus in a certain sense they coincide.

Because individual judgment and the Last Judgment coincide, at the Last Judgment every man stands before the seat of the divine Judge and "experiences" the event of the Last Judgment, which exceeds all human measure. But participation in the Last Judgment, which encompasses all men, is also a sign that the judged soul can leave the earthly state only through the center of the human state and must witness the separation of all human possibilities into good and evil.

7

Of Paradise and Hell

In a rudimentary and one-sided picture, one can imagine the blessed and the damned as two multitudes surrounding God in many circles: the blessed with their gaze directed[3] towards the luminous Center, the damned on the contrary with their gaze directed outwards towards the darkness. The closer a blessed soul stands to God, the greater its rapture, but the closer a damned soul stands to God, the greater the field of its somber vision and the more abysmal its despair. In this picture Lucifer, the fallen angel of the light, would stand closest to God and yet be the furthest from Him; for is not the sacrilege of turning one's back upon God the more appalling, the closer one is standing to Him? (In Islam it is said that Satan has his throne between Heaven and earth.)

---

3 In German, *richten*, which, as the author proceeds to say in the original text, has the double meaning of looking in a certain direction and of being judged. —Translator

One would need to introduce a third group into this picture: the penitents, whose gaze is indeed directed towards the Center, but whose sins rise up like a mountain before them and obstruct their view of God. This would be purgatory, corresponding in the next world to remorse in this world. The divine Rays ultimately cause the mountain to melt.

The damned wished themselves to be God; they shall be taken at their word, and burdened with all the loneliness that only God can bear. Only God, Who is in the Center, can look outward to the abyss without being engulfed by it.

Creatures, which are outside, must look inwards, into the Center, otherwise the horror of the infernally deep shadow of their own poor, empty soul overcomes them.

The symbolism of being judged in the double meaning of the word[4] appears in various places, e.g., in the saga of Orpheus, in which the singer, contravening the divine injunction, turns to look back at his wife, who is following him out of the underworld but must in consequence return to Hades; or in the tale of Lot's wife, who looked back at Sodom as it was being destroyed, and was turned into a pillar of salt.

4 That is, directing one's gaze and being judged; see preceding note. —Translator

In the ninth song of the *Divine Comedy* Dante meets the Medusa, whose gaze turns men to stone. Virgil commands Dante to turn back for his own safety and to cover his eyes; indeed he holds Dante's eyes closed with his own hands. The following verse of Dante hints that a profound mystery is being touched upon:

O ye who have undistempered intellects,
Observe the teaching that is concealed
Beneath the veil of my strange verses!

Man can reflect with impunity upon the eternity of hell, but if he looks directly into the abyss of this eternity in its full reality, he is, as a contingent being, no match for its overwhelming power; in an inversion of spiritual rapture he loses his temporality and becomes a stone imprisoned in itself eternally—in the infernal sense of the term, this is the Medusa's gaze. To become petrified with horror is a faint earthly presentiment of this state.

It is told of Muhammad that he never turned around while walking; this was so well-known that his companions used to converse unabashedly behind him. This habit, too, is connected with the symbolism of the direction of the gaze.

From a universal standpoint, of course, beatitude and damnation are cancelled out, since God alone is real. Thus there is hope for the damned, presupposing that they look towards the Center. Earth, Heaven, and hell must finally shatter before God—indeed, totally; they do not end, rather, they never began.

The scriptures describe Paradise and hell both for the guidance of believers and in praise of God, in order that He may appear in the total Compassion and the total Rigor of His Absoluteness.

At first man loves God's Mercy and fears His Rigor. More profoundly, however, he fears His Mercy also, since it is awesome in its unimaginable greatness, and he loves His Rigor since it is just and arises from paternal solicitude for man and his free will; this inversion of relationships explains the confusing sentence inscribed over Dante's hell: "I was created by the Omnipotence of God, by highest Wisdom and first Love."

Second Meditation

❖ ❖ ❖

Of the Resurrection of the Flesh

1

Investiture of Light and Dark Forces in Human Bodies

It is said that on the Day of Judgment the Word of God will enter the scene as a witness, in the figure of a man; the world, which has seduced men, also appears on the Day of Judgment in the guise of a hideous woman (the title "frow werlde" [Madame World] in Middle High German poetry and her description as beautiful in front and a mass of serpents behind, is by no means only a poetic inspiration); it is well-known that the angels and Satan are also present in human form.

This investiture of light and dark forces on Judgment Day is richly instructive: it means that what befell man in life was at bottom his own creation and was formed after his own image.

That image of the world which enters a man's consciousness is real for him. So many impressions crowd in from outside that, according to our tendencies or insights, we involuntarily close the door of our consciousness to most of them, yet allow some to enter; thus two people can experience the same environment in fundamentally different ways.

Forms based upon divine revelations imbue human consciousness with those impressions which allow us to feel the proximity of God, e.g., through temples symbolic in their construction, noble garments, well-ordered morals, and profound prayer forms, etc., whereas they attempt to maintain at a distance those impressions that divert us from seeing God; but in contrast, a merely human, worldly culture deliberately steers our attention towards the world and its distractions. The man living under the protection of a theocentric culture feels the nearness of God and becomes so attuned to the language of divine signs that he begins to understand them immediately, just as a child starts to understand human language by imitating its parents.

Before the Fall, Adam did not admit the duality good and evil into his consciousness, and thus he stood beyond Judgment, in Paradise. But fallen man grants entry to this duality and is thus subject to Judgment.

If one considers that man has the capacity to create his own worlds full of innocence or guilt, on the basis of what he does or does not allow to enter his consciousness, one measures—or at least has a presentiment of—the greatness of one's responsibility on Judgment Day. There are countless worlds. With each man's death, one of these perishes and is judged.

From the Christian point of view, the divine Word appears on the Day of Judgment in the figure of Christ as Judge of the worlds. In Islam, too, the sages teach that on the Day of Reckoning the Koran will become manifest as a beautiful youth.

> And so on the day of Resurrection the Koran comes in the figure of a man of beautiful countenance and character: he intercedes for us, and his intercession is granted! (Al-Ghazali, *The Precious Pearl of the Hereafter*).

The mystery of Christ's body (the holy transubstantiation at the Last Supper), the mystery of angelic bodies, and finally the mystery of the resurrection of the flesh are closely connected with the significance that the body has for the human soul. On one hand the body is a part of our soul, a state of our consciousness. Only insofar as we are conscious of it—in some manner or another—does the body exist for us. By means of sight and touch, by heat, cold, weight, tension, and many other sensations the body is transformed into a content of our consciousness (and to be complete, one must add that a portion of earthly actualities lying outside our body enter our consciousness also, through the portal of our body or the doors of the senses).

Certain phenomena occurring in dreams show clearly that the body is a state of consciousness; if the dreamer were not to bear his body in his consciousness, how could he then clothe his "I" with it and have it move around thus, while his real body, i.e., that of which he is conscious when awake, lies sunk in sleep? On the other hand, however, the body belongs to the earthly world and is thus opposed to the soul in a certain way.

2

Body and Self-Knowledge

The soul is aware of the body, but as an alien state, as an "exterior." Because the body is simultaneously soul and something other than soul, it can hold up to the soul an image of itself, as an illuminated mirror throws back the light that strikes it.

The soul finds itself portrayed by the body; reflecting upon the form and structure of the human body can be a key to the soul's self-knowledge. Thus, for example, the three circulatory systems: food, breath, and blood, correspond among other things (the correspondences are in truth innumerable!) to the three ways of aspiring to God, namely good works, divine Love, and divine Knowledge. Think of the flesh and blood of Christ at the Last Supper: the flesh or bread (the food) symbolizes the fulfillment of the Law, or good works, and the blood, which flows out of and returns to the heart-center, is the sacred, intoxicating wine of divine Knowledge, a knowledge which in this case also includes love; for he who "knows" God (if we may venture this expression: it is an ellipsis for the highest human knowledge, though holding in reserve the unfathomable profundity of God)—he who knows God, also loves Him. Knowledge brings about Union, and Union brings about Love. (The oneness of Knowledge and Love is expressed on the human plane by the fine old saying: "he knew his wife," in which once again the symbolic imagery of the physical act becomes evident.)

It is immediately intelligible that the breath stands for love; think of its warming and dilating power, in contrast to which suffocation corresponds to lovelessness. Perhaps we may be reminded also of the role played by the wind, "the breath of nature," as disseminator in the love life of plants.

If man becomes conscious of the meaning of his body (in the sense of a flash of spiritual insight into the body's language), the sacredness of the flesh becomes accessible to him. The man oriented exclusively outwards—very frequent today—is however unable to connect his body with the Inward, he must rather accept it as the ultimate dimension, i.e., he inevitably confuses the body with the soul. He takes the body, which is only an outermost limit of our consciousness, for the whole.

No wonder, then, that death, the dissolution of the body, is for him the end of his life, indeed, the end of every existence! But he for whom the body is a reflection of the Inward cannot take physical death for the perishing of the soul: a content of consciousness vanishes, but consciousness itself remains. Certainly, the interweaving of consciousness with the body is so dense and ramified that the separation during and after the dying process is like the uprooting of a tree established deeply and broadly in the soil: it is neither effortless nor simple. Thus one soul, as if shivering, may wander about looking for the lost garment of the body, while another, dying after an agonizing, patiently-borne suffering, or passing to the next world through a death offered as a spiritual sacrifice, may be able to release itself more easily; there are as many destinies in this regard as there are human beings.

To what extent can it be arduous even for the spiritual man to take leave of the world? Answer:

insofar as the world is a manifestation of God and not merely world, the spiritual man, too, loves it; indeed, his love for the world is more profound than that of the purely profane man.

Life is a dying; death is only the last step; thank God if death has time to mature us, slowly, tranquilly, and completely! Or if a man has already died in the Spirit before he dies physically, i.e., if he has turned his soul entirely inwards instead of outwards, and thus withdrawn it from the body.

3

Of the Resurrection of the Flesh

How must one understand the resurrection of the flesh, the re-furnishing of the deceased with his former body on the Day of Judgment?

The resurrection of the flesh can be understood from the point of view of the end of time, the Last Judgment, the Instant (*Nu*), since all of "time," or more precisely "our entire temporal cycle," with all it ever contained, will withdraw into Non-Time.

At that moment human consciousness will be mirrored anew in the body belonging to it; however, as this consciousness has been transformed since death, so, too, the mirror-image will be different from what it was in life; the blessed will have from then on a paradisal body corresponding to their beatified state, and the damned, an infernal body corresponding to their damnation.

The skeptics constantly ask how it is possible for each soul to find its body again on the Day of Judgment, since the material of our body returns to general circulation after death and may serve for the construction of a new body. They forget that the body is a state of consciousness, and that, for example, we also possess a body in our dreams, without "material" being necessary for its formation.

One could also adduce that the world was created from the *Nu*, from the Instant, like a flash of lightning, and that this provenance from the divine Instant is manifested in the temporal domain by the fact that the world is created completely anew at every "point in time." God is the Creator eternally, not only at the "beginning" of the world (which cannot exist, from the "temporal" point of view), and the world is thus completely fresh and original in each instant; in this lies its profundity. The temporal cohesion of the world, composed of cause and effect, is an illusion; in truth this apparent cohesion consists of a succession of closely proximate but mutually unconnected "points in time." Matter, too, is by no means something continually reused to make new bodies, but rather a dense succession of innumerable divine creations, for which reason all bodies can be resurrected independently of one another at the Last Judgment.

Let us add yet another observation. Just as the human body is a state of human consciousness, so, too, the whole physical world is a state of "cosmic consciousness" or rather, the consciousness of the "Lord of the worlds"—designating a certain aspect of God. The human body is simultaneously a state of individual consciousness and a state of cosmic consciousness; the two aspects coincide during earthly life and again on the Day of Judgment. And just as human consciousness, when it dreams, can bring forth not just one, but many bodies, so, too, cosmic consciousness in the "dream-substantial"[1] state that lies behind the physical world—the Creator's own atelier—has the power to bring forth as many bodies as It pleases. The bodies "dreamed" by the individual consciousness are seen only by the individual; those "dreamed" by the cosmic consciousness can in principle be seen by the whole world.

1 That is, the subtle realm in which the cosmic Dreamer "dreams" the archetypal forms which are then created or actualized on the physical plane. —Translator

Just as one loaf (symbol of the body) sufficed to feed ten thousand, so, too, a little "flesh" is enough to clothe innumerable souls at the Last Judgment.

4

Human Body and Universal Man

Insofar as Christ was the son "of man," i.e., Universal Man, the cosmic consciousness belonged to him; the whole physical world, therefore, was his body, and he could thus, in the most literal sense of the word, and by no means only metaphorically, refer to bread and wine as his flesh and blood. (By the way, even the ordinary man's consciousness of his own body radiates into his environment; and at a certain stage of spiritualization, man experiences the ground upon which he walks, the air he breathes, the sky above him etc., indeed, the people he encounters, as belonging to his own body. One need only imagine this spiritual "incorporation," endlessly expanded and deepened, to grasp what is meant by the notion of "Universal Man.")

In the miracle of the Resurrection Christ created his body anew out of the cosmic consciousness, just as on the Day of Judgment the bodies of the dead will be created out of it.

When man admits into his consciousness "superhuman" states that soar high above earthly ones, beyond forms and in a word "angelic," these states or angels can in certain cases assume human form in order to bring messages from the next world; to contest these possibilities is by no means a sign of "enlightenment," but on the contrary a consequence of these states being denied entrance to human consciousness today. (By the way, the angels can also choose the form of animals; the whale in whose belly the Prophet Jonah was rescued may have been an angelic manifestation of this kind.)

The fallen angel Satan, too, can appear as a man; he dislikes doing so, since the frightful ugliness and villainous baseness of his appearance testify against him, but he can be forced to show himself by the ever-vigilant warning powers of a spiritualized human consciousness. It is a bad sign for an epoch when the devil knows how to remain invisible, or even succeeds in being publicly declared non-existent. What could serve his evil intentions better?

In many legends it is told that the devil appeared in an outwardly beautiful, seductive form, as a sweetly smiling, handsome man or an attractive woman; however, this is not his own appearance, but rather a mask he employs, drawn from the suppressed wish-dreams of men.

5

Image and Reality of Judgment

On the Day of Judgment the angels gather in a multitude around the throne of God, and Satan, too, the fallen angel, makes himself known, with terrible grimaces and repulsive deformations, and surrounded by his helpers. It may seem childish to visualize this image in earthly, corporeal terms—and the reality of the Last Judgment is certainly different than man can paint it during life, and in truth completely inconceivable—yet this immediately graspable, naive imagining has something correct in it which every purely conceptual interpretation lacks; for even if they appear in forms completely different than we expect, it is a question of the resurrection of these bodies of ours that actually exist today, and by no means a merely illustrative manner of expression for a non-physical event. Similarly, the light and dark powers clothe themselves in bodies that are just as comprehensible, and convince us just as directly, as the human body we possess in life.

The visible and perceptible world in which we live is "the here-below" or the "world" only from a superficial point of view: in its veritable nature it is a creation of God, a divine revelation and a divine manifestation. It is the language in which God deigned to speak with men, and God will scarcely be disloyal to this language in order to avail Himself all of a sudden of the pale discourse of a so-called "metaphysician," after having created stars, mountains, plants and, animals.

Also, one must not forget that when God speaks for example of the fruits in Paradise, or of other joys that are familiar to us from earthly life, He consecrates these fruits and joys for us already in earthly life, and opens our understanding to their profound, celestial meaning; and when He speaks of the tortures of hell in images that remind us of earthly diseases or pains, He teaches us in what sense we can spiritualize these trials in our present life.

If the assembled souls are re-furnished with bodies at the Last Judgment, it happens thus because (as we saw earlier) the state of consciousness which is the body is a mirror to man, in which he recognizes his own image (just as the world is a mirror, in which God recognizes Himself: "And God saw what He had made, and behold, it was good" [Genesis 1:31]).

The Judgment would be incomplete if those who are judged did not recognize themselves and were not obliged to confirm the Judge's verdict; one can understand beatitude as an enjoyment by the blessed of the beauty of their own soul, and damnation as the suffering of the damned due to the ugliness of their soul—but the body holds up to them a mirror image of the beauty or ugliness of their soul.

6

Of the Sacredness of the Body

For many who struggle against the idea of the resurrection of the flesh, the despising of the body plays a role. Is it not something unspiritual, dense, and blind? Should it last forever? These despisers of the body forget that God accomplishes a miracle even out of dust. God does not consider it beneath His dignity to pass through the portal of the body, and this in both directions: inwards, by making His divine Word enter through man's physical ear, and the image of the divine creation pass through his physical eye; and outwards, by having divine truths proclaimed through the mouth of man, and realized by his limbs.

The divine determination leaves its imprint on the body and the body's parts: the positioning of the ears far on the outside of the head and yet at the same time upon the passages that lead to the center, as well as the inward-turning spiral form of the cochlea, both reflect the equilibrium between circumference and center, between the all-embracing and the all-uniting (by the Center), that also characterizes the divine Word. (The animal ear often tapers to a point and can be flexed, thus indicating a point, a center, that is situated externally.) Let us also mention that in the primordial Hindu word AUM (Om), the A corresponds to the straight line, the U to an arc, and the M to a point, which once again is in conformity with the spiral form of the cochlea, or, in another domain, the bishop's crosier. These indications illustrate the connection between the human ear and the divine Word.

And the opening of the radiating eye constantly repeats on the human plane the divine command at the Creation: "Let there be light!" while the eye's closing is a physical indication of spiritual "Un-Becoming," the sacred way inwards, as against the way of Creation; it points to the *nox profunda*, the night of Non-Being, the undifferentiated divine Ground. When we pray or meditate, our eyes close as if of their own accord.

The revelation of divine Truths leaves its seal in the form of the human speech organ. "And the Spirit of God moved upon the face of the waters" (Genesis 1:2). Is the breath that carries the words not a direct symbol of the divine Spirit? And the mouth with its wavy lips, the tongue with its billowing movement, the soft cheeks and the stream of saliva, are they not a direct symbol of "the waters"? i.e., the possibilities from which the Spirit chooses what It wishes to summon to life? And the diverse "densities" of the sounds, from the light breath of an H and the varying degrees of articulation of the other consonants, to the full voice of the vowels: are these not direct symbols of that succession of sheaths with which, according to the Hindus, Atma progressively clothes itself, bringing forth in this manner the series of worlds, from the realm of that which is situated before all form, to the subtle realm, and so to the corporeal realm (to name only three principal degrees)?

Human limbs, too, reveal in their form and movement the divine determination for which they are intended, namely the realization of divine truths. One thinks of the hand with the five rays of the fingers, an image of radiating divine blessing; or of walking, symbol of divine creation, in that when we move ahead, new spaces are always opening up before us, just as in duration creation follows upon creation from moment to moment. At each step, movement flows from the center, namely the body's center of gravity, and it is only this flow from the center that bestows unity upon our steps, which, seen outwardly from the ground, follow in regular succession but always at an interval; the swinging of the walking legs corresponds to the knowledge that the unfolding of the world is only seemingly continuous, but in truth is produced by a sequence of countless small, mutually independent instants or steps, each flashing from the Center. The rhythm of walking is transmitted outwards from the center of gravity; the center participates in a more intense manner in dance, where the feet only cursorily touch the floor. No wonder that there are sacred dances which represent Shiva as Creator of the world. When walking and dancing we are seized by the rhythm of the center, which rhythm can in certain circumstances fill us with superhuman powers.

7

Of the Paradisal and the Infernal Body

The body is the gateway between the interior and the exterior. Yet what is the interior, fundamentally, but the "I," or rather, the "Self," for the "I" is still largely determined from outside? And what is the exterior, fundamentally, but "He"? One could also designate the interior as the domain of freedom and the exterior as the domain of necessity: inwardly we have the free deployment of the Self and outwardly, the world such as fate has willed it.

A soul striving inward increasingly approaches freedom, a soul losing itself in the exterior falls further under the sway of necessity—or, since the significance of this is no longer apparent from within—under the sway of blind coercion. (A world view oriented outward, such as materialism, leads ineluctably to coercion in the political domain; sin, too, which always includes an "exteriorization," is invariably connected with coercion; think of the sway of habit in the case of vices. In each sin an aspect of human nature exercises coercion over the other aspects: in gluttony, the stomach is lord; in the case of pride, the feeling of "I" sets itself up as ruler; with avarice, it is the sense of possession; with extravagance, the underestimation of values, etc.)

At the Last Judgment both the soul that strove inward and the soul that dispersed itself in the external world will find their former bodies again, however the reunion with them is accomplished under inverse premises. The body being resurrected at the end of time contains all the possibilities that it has unfolded within time (and also those that it could not unfold). All these possibilities are there "simultaneously," ready to be grasped by the soul. The body being resurrected has in other words the plasticity of the fruit in the womb. After death the soul that has tended towards inner freedom takes from these physical possibilities those congenial to it. The paradisal body is an expression of greater freedom than the earthly body. If we wish to describe its attributes we must draw upon conditions familiar to us in this world; they would be transferable to the corresponding circumstances in the next world, for which human imagination and words are lacking. The paradisal body is less bound by gravity, so that it can soar into the heights (this attribute also characterizing the bodies of saints).

It is a telling symbol that on other planets, which can represent worlds in the hereafter, the body weighs more or less than it does on earth, due to greater or lesser gravitational fields. On one hand the sun is a symbol of truth and life-giving mercy because of its light and warmth. On the other hand, as a place, it is an image of hell, of eternal fire, because of its scorching heat and great mass which would give the body—were it to escape incineration—an unimaginable weight. And this interpretation holds further, in that the damned soul is in fact enclosed in the Truth, but suffers it as an eternal negation of itself. One thinks of the fall of Icarus, who flew too close to the sun, or of the fall of Phaeton when he sought to drive the solar chariot.

The experience of weight is connected with that of fear and powerlessness; when one is greatly frightened one's limbs can become leaden. But for this reason the increase of weight can also be a good omen, namely an accompaniment to an increase in spiritual awe in connection with God's proximity. One recalls St. Christopher, who carried the Christ child across the water, and with each step had more weight to bear, until finally the whole world was upon his shoulders. And tradition relates of Muhammad that when he received the revelations his body became as heavy as lead. Under the weight of the divine Word, even his riding camel often fell to its knees.

Incidentally, there is a correspondence between this camel and St. Christopher. The camel is a symbol of the seeker of God: it lives in the desert, whither hermits withdraw; it is poor and needs nothing, like a fakir (the Arabic *faqir* means "one who is poor"); it also senses when its rider allows it to go freely towards the next well—this corresponds to the sense for sacred blessing; in the midst of dryness it has a reserve of water, just as the spiritual seeker carries a source of eternal wisdom in his heart in the midst of the desert of the world; and it serves man as a humble mount, just as St. Christopher carried travelers across a ford to the glory of God. The servant's burden is a spiritual weight; the divine meaning of his service is revealed when Christ (thus the Word of God) or the Koran (again the Word of God) has become this weight. Carrying travelers through the desert or across a river is a symbol of priesthood, of the function of teacher or master. Priests, teachers, or masters rescue souls as they traverse the world.

Unlike the physical body, the paradisal one is not bound to a "Here," it can be in various places simultaneously; this capacity, too, has been demonstrated in the case of saints who were seen in the same moment in various places. The paradisal body is not subject to time: it enjoys eternal youth. (According to Anne Catherine Emmerich, the body of the Blessed Virgin resembled that of a girl, remaining youthful to the last.)

Ultimately the consciousness of spiritual freedom radiates right into the *materia* of the paradisal body. As limit of physical consciousness, it will be aware— albeit in a completely material manner—of its nature as soul; in order to be transformed into soul, matter is sacrificed, so to speak, and this is manifested by an exceedingly fresh, pure fragrance (I would say akin to lily-of-the-valley) that emanates from it. (In spring the plants are seized by Love, and Love is sacrifice; from the blossoms then emanates that mysterious fragrance that recalls the dissolution of matter, its transformation into soul. Similarly, the sanctity of the soul can render the body fragrant: not uncommonly a perfume issues from the graves of saints or from their remains.)

Inversely, a stench is associated with the infernal body. Instead of the auto-transformation of matter into soul, this stench corresponds on the contrary to the dragging down of the animic substance by matter. When, for example, the image imprinted on the body by the soul disintegrates into inert matter, as happens with the decomposition of the corpse, noisome odors are released; even fouler vapors are produced when a soul that is materialized through and through returns to its body on the Day of Judgment—it would putrefy, were it not held together by the same curse that prevents even damned souls from escaping into a non-existence.

The exteriorized soul is afflicted above all by confusing the body with itself; it seeks freedom externally and believes that the compulsion to do so is situated within, in its conscience, in spiritual exigence. After death—succumbing to a dreadful inadvertence[2]— it chooses from the plenitude of possibilities of the resurrected body those which fit into the narrow frame of its hallucinations; it takes measurements for its own infernal body, which is to the earthly body as a prison cell is to a garden, indeed a cell in which one can neither stand upright, nor stretch out, nor sit comfortably, and in which one must remain until being delivered by divine Grace.

2 As the author points out in the original text, the German word *Versehen* (inadvertence) literally means an inversion or distortion of the correct vision. —Translator

Third Meditation

⊕ ⊕ ⊕

Earthly Signs of Heaven

1

Of the Unity of the Earthly Dream

The world is like a dream of God, dreamed by Him in His capacity as Lord of the worlds; man's life, and the life of the other beings, are dreams within this general dream; the end of time is like an awakening from the world dream, the death of beings is like an awakening from their individual dream.

Amnesia is a hallmark of the world; sooner or later it engulfs all events. But, in contrast, the memory remains of the fact that the world is just a dream—this memory is religion (= re-binding)— or in other words the memory of the waking state (= divine Revelation). This consciousness of the dream nature of the world must be present in its center, as the all-governing principle, till the end.

If we consider the world as a dream, we are naturally thinking only remotely of the human dream, which is often arbitrary, deliquescent, meaningless; the divine dream on the other hand, i.e., the world, reflects the attributes of its Originator; it is profound, grave, full of immeasurable wisdom, but also full of gaiety, beauty and an inconceivable wealth of inspiration.

If one considers the world as a great revolving sphere, and people and other living beings as many small revolving spheres, one must realize that all these revolving spheres can in truth have only one Center, namely God; all other centers, apparently independent of Him, have only the degree of reality of mirror images in relation to Him. Thus the "I," which is seemingly our center, is in truth only a fragmented reflection of the Self, i.e., of our other-worldly Origin, reposing in God and ultimately inseparable from Him.

Similarly, what the other beings feel to be their center-point is in reality only a reflection of the veritable divine Center-point, namely the "Idea"—if one may use this word—that underlies these beings and is not separate from God.

By perceiving each other, beings testify that behind them all lies a common Center that shines through the apparent centers and re-amalgamates on a profound level that which is superficially separate. The German greeting *Gruss Gott* (God be greeted [in thee]) is deeply significant, since the divine Center lives in both of those meeting, and thus God in fact greets Himself. The meaning of neighborly love, too, lies in the fact that the common Namer of I and thou is God. And the Sufi saying (attributed to Muhammad): "He who knows himself, knows his Lord" is founded upon the coincidence of the human center with the Center of the worlds.

2

Of the Mystery of External Things

The man oriented outwards sees a welcome diversion from his own soul and its exhorting call in the beings who encounter him during his existence, and in the world that surrounds him: he flees into the distraction of the varied and colorful outer world.

In contrast, the inwardly-directed man recognizes other beings and his environment as reflections of realities that exist within him, behind the "I," in the divine Self. The other beings and the environment are thus no diversion, but on the contrary, supports for concentration upon the true Center that lies behind his "I."

For these two ways of considering external things, one may quote the saying of the Redeemer:

The light of the body is the eye. If therefore thine eye be single, thy whole body shall be full of light. But if thine eye be evil, thy whole body shall be full of darkness. If therefore the light that is in thee be darkness, how great is that darkness! (Matthew 6:22-23)

He who can think back to how he saw the world in the innocence of early childhood, remembers that all beings and things were as if surrounded by a radiance. This mystery of beings and things is real, and consists in their reflecting something that is deep within, hidden in our own soul.

A hermit who had lived for decades in the forest no longer knew how his own face looked. But one day, between the tree trunks, a face met him that was mysteriously foreign to him and yet looked at him familiarly: it was his own, held up to him by the mirror of an expanse of water. Thus do external things show the inwardly-oriented man his forgotten spiritual countenance.

3

Of Symbols for the States after Death

We call the homeland of the blessed "Heaven." And indeed, in a child or an interiorized man, the vision of the earthly canopy of heaven immediately evokes an experience of beatitude. The blueness of the sky is like a mysterious curtain veiling immeasurable radiance; the height and breadth of the heavenly vault remind us of the loftiness and freedom of the liberated soul. The stars are angels or Names of God, the rain is His purifying and nourishing Mercy (this divine rain or blessing is answered by man's tears of remorse), the thunder is His Word, the clouds are His thoughts.

> Then went up Moses, and Aaron, Nadab and Abihu, and seventy of the elders of Israel; And they saw the God of Israel; and there was under his feet as it were a paved work of a sapphire stone, and as it were the body of Heaven in his clearness. (Exodus 24:9-10)

The thought of hell is bound just as cogently with images of abysses and the craters of fire-spewing mountains. Imprisonment in low, dark mine tunnels in which one can progress only gropingly, corresponds to the constriction of damned souls (one thinks of the etymological connection between *Enge* [narrowness] and *Angst* [fear]!);[1] the fire in the earth's interior represents the "eternal fire," the crushing weight

---

1 Compare the English word "anguish" and the Latin word from which it derives, *angustus* (narrow). —Translator

of the earth's crust symbolizes the overwhelming pressure; isolation from daylight makes us think of the hopelessness of the damned; and the sojourn in depths where no living thing flourishes, of their dreadful abandonment.

4

Of Animals as Messengers of the Hereafter

The eagle is the bird of heaven. It is not for nothing that it is sacred to Zeus, and the symbol of the apostle John. It flies the highest of our indigenous birds. Let us transfer ourselves into it, with our full imaginative capacity, when, visible from the earth only as a dot, it circles at improbable height, solitary, still, tiny in comparison to the depth beneath it, its wings outstretched to the last feather; then we sense the beatitude of flight, to which we cannot in any way compare the sensation of a man artificially propelled into the sky.

The "conquest of the air" by man is indeed only a further step in outward evasion, whereas the eagle in its tireless circling indicates on the contrary a single point in the canopy of heaven, as if announcing to us the existence of a divine Center at the zenith of the heavenly vault.

The altitude of the eagle's flight is a symbol of the proximity of God; the acuity of its gaze, with which it espies the smallest living creature on the ground, is a symbol of the divine Omniscience; the breadth of its soaring and the rapacious grip of its beak and talons are symbols of the combination of all-inclusiveness and centrality in God.

The interpretation of the eagle, just as that of Heaven, is no poetic invention. The divine Creation is a language; created realities such as heaven or eagle are God's words just as much as the scriptural parables or sayings. The primordial, uncorrupted man reads the book of the world just as naturally as a revealed text. Concerning the eagle, John G. Neihardt, for example, tells us in his fine book *Black Elk Speaks* that the great Native American visionary Black Elk held up an eagle feather and said: "This means *Wakan Tanka* (the Great Mysterious One); and it also means that our thoughts should rise high as the eagles do."

5

Individual Being and Essential Being

Much more encompassing than the eagle as an individual being or species is "eagle-hood," i.e., the archetype or original divine Idea "eagle," which finds its strongest expression amongst earthly beings as an eagle bird (though also manifested in other birds and animals), yet flashes out in the most diverse domains within humanity, e.g., in particular prophets and saints such as the apostle John or Dante Alighieri, men whose soul was cut to the aquiline model.

Dante was aquiline in his very appearance; and spiritually, too, he soared aloft like an eagle through infernal, purgatorial, and heavenly circles to the throne of God. As a poet, and in his tenacious holding to his mighty vision, he demonstrated the power of the eagle's grip.

John's aquiline proximity to God was already shown in his lying on the breast of the Lord; the Apocalypse is filled with aquiline soaring, to an even higher degree than the *Divine Comedy*. We also find heavenly flight akin to that of an eagle in Muhammad's Night Journey, which brought him to Allah's throne; this story has been considered a model for the *Divine Comedy*, though it is forgotten that neither of these is a work of literature, they are both the result of direct celestial vision.

In the book *Of the Twelve Teachers*, St. Hieronymus writes of St. Augustine:

Augustine the bishop flew like an eagle over the mountain peaks; he did not look at what lay at the foot of the mountains, but measured the breadth of heaven and revealed the position of the earth and the circle of the waters from above, in luminous language.

In a broader sense one can count all true seekers of God among the eagles: Jakob Böhme flew twice over Heaven in a rapture lasting for days; the above-mentioned Native American visionary Black Elk was transported to Heaven during a long trance. But ultimately, the aquiline quality is placed in every man's heart: the sight of the visible eagle can help to call this into awareness.

The other birds, right down to the sparrow, are in a certain respect also eagles, or rather, modifications thereof. The lark, for instance, although it does not fly as high as the eagle, expresses the beatitude and ecstasy of the soul attaining Paradise by its whirring, vertical ascent and jubilant song; morning, which it loves especially, is of course a general symbol for the dawning of beatitude after the end of the earthly night.

The antithesis of the matutinal trilling lark is the melodiously sighing nightingale: here night no longer has the sense of earthly darkness, it is the *nox profunda*, the abyssal night of the seeker of

God, the extinguishing of the world before God; the nightingale's song expresses the innermost yearning of the soul and its flowing into God.

If one reflects that each tree is an image of the world axis, i.e., the vertical dimension which opens in the center of the horizontal world towards the upper and also the lower worlds (the gates to Paradise and hell are adjacent), and if one reflects further that the branches of the tree symbolize the higher and lower worlds in the hierarchy of the universe, one comprehends that the song birds are like saved souls which are no longer caught in one specific world, but move freely among the most diverse spiritual, animic, and physical states. The scale upon which their songs are based is a further symbol of this possibility of untrammeled wandering through the hierarchy of innumerable realms.

We would think it contradictory or "tasteless" if the eagle were given the voice of a songbird: it is at the zenith, abiding in God's proximity, and correspondingly its shrill cry is absolute, without gradation.

6

Animals as Manifesters of Mystery

Apart from the bird kingdom, thousands of other living beings manifest mysteries that lie not only outside but simultaneously within our own soul. Just as behind the eagle there is a much more encompassing "eagle-hood" which can be manifested in many ways, so, too, behind each animal, plant, and rock there is an essence which can be manifested in entirely different forms, above all in certain attributes of the human soul.

Astrology looms large in the present day, like a ruined monument that we no longer understand; but when animal names were given to particular constellations, e.g., the "Little Bear" and the "Great Bear," this arose from the vision of the archetype of these animals—thus for example of "bear-hood"—of which one knew that they were more than merely an animal species: namely, a universal principle; otherwise how could they have been rediscovered in the night sky?

Due to the combination of massive strength with equally great agility that characterizes it, but above all due to its appearance and behavior, the rounded, majestic form of its head and body, and the round—as if embracing—yet lightning power of its movements, which give it the circumspection of a patriarch or chief, the bear was the royal animal for the Celts, whereas the boar was attributed to the Druids, by virtue of its solitariness. It is no accident that the bear became extinct in the West at the same time as the aristocracy fell into decadence and dissolution in society; the connection between a particular animal archetype and a spiritual attribute in man is often reflected in a historical parallelism.

From this point of view, the extinction of so many animal species in our time is not unconnected with the equally evident impoverishment of inner spiritual possibilities in man. The gradual disappearance of the eagle from our regions is indicative; and the perishing of mighty species like the bison, the elk, the Atlas lion, etc. goes hand in hand with a dwarfism of the average human soul.

If the cow is sacred to the Hindus, the bison to the Native Americans, the Apis bull to the Egyptians, it is because these peoples see in the particular animal only the expression of a much more general essence that is manifested also in the human soul and beyond, into the next world; the drawings of cave-dwellers touched upon these divine archetypes also.

The herds of cattle or bison move like nomads, according to pasture; they flee the narrow, the limited, like the spiritual seeker who has no place to lay his head. They are at peace with all creatures and are sufficiently nourished by grass; the sweetness and soft fullness of their milk is pure mercy. They confront evil, the enemy that attacks them, like a knight, head on, with lowered horns; this is a symbol of spiritual immediacy, the straight path; victory or defeat issues from their forehead just as Athena, goddess of wisdom, issued from the head of Zeus. The bull's disdain of death and its combative fury are like the qualities with which a saint vanquishes his own ego. (The bull which engages the spiritual center incarnated by the torero and perishes in sanguinary ecstasy is not to be pitied by comparison with other bulls, but envied. A fight and death of this kind is completely prefigured in the nature of the bull, and is no more an animal torture than the sacred sacrifice of animals, e.g., in the case of the Israelites).

The representation of Moses with a horned head may be traceable to an incorrect translation of the Vulgate, but a profound meaning underlies it nevertheless: in Moses' case horns are a mark of the connection with worlds which unfold above man's head, thus above what he can comprehend with his mind. But then one thinks also of the nomadic nature of cattle; during their wandering in the desert Moses transformed the Jews into a nomadic people.

Just as we have attributed "eagle-hood" to all birds, so, too, all horned animals qualify for bull-hood. Let us take the ram! Not only does the spiral of its horns point inwards, but the line over its nose and mouth also runs inwards, reminiscent of the visionary profile of certain Semitic heads; the animal is moreover nestled in wool like the embryonic chick in the egg-yolk; all expresses interiority, center, warmth, peace, innocence. Even if one knew nothing about the role of the lamb as Easter sacrifice, one would understand why Christ has been characterized as the Lamb of God; with its centrality goes the fact that the ram is the animal of the Origin, the beginning (just as Aries in the zodiac represents the beginning of spring).

Horns are always a kind of crown, whether they open upwards like a half-moon in which the divine Mother might stand (the Apis bull is often portrayed with a white half-moon on its chest), or curve inwards like a bishop's crosier (the shepherd's crook was made like a ram's horn from profound knowledge); they reflect the connection with the higher or—what amounts to the same—the inner, paradisal states; this is also the case with the stag's antlers, whose ramification corresponds to the ladder of the worlds, just as the branches of a tree do.

The stag bears as it were the triple crown of the pope. As applied to the stag, the forest symbolizes the universe, and the lower and higher branches are symbols of the lower and higher, earthly and celestial realms within the universe. The possession of antlers—the crown of a tree in miniature, so to speak!—can then only be a symbol that a being has realized the lower and higher universal states within itself. Thus it is no wonder that in medieval pictorial language, the stag symbolizes universal Man and Jesus Christ.

The phenomenon of a white stag with a cross between its antlers arises as a consequence of the stag archetype, though it is irrelevant here whether it is a question of a flesh-and-blood stag or an angelic or visionary expression of "stag-hood." In the legend of St. Eustace, it is Christ himself who assumes the figure of the hunted stag and speaks to his pursuer in order to convert him.

Is there a nobler symbol of spiritual humility than the stag when it arches back its neck and head, so that its antlers press against its rump, enabling it to traverse a thicket? In its distress it looks heavenward and so to speak lays aside its proud crown, like a saint who prays to God like a child, as if he did not bear a heavenly treasure of wisdom and virtue in his heart, or like Christ, who suffered on the cross, though he was

God Himself. How often one sees, on old carpets and in miniatures, the stag with its neck arched back—it is so to speak the heraldic animal of the spiritual man caught in the thicket of the world; the spiritual man must hide his grandeur in order not to perish. It is no accident that the Psalmist chose the stag yearning for fresh water as a symbol of the spiritual seeker.

If the stag represents Christ, it is not surprising that the Blessed Virgin is depicted with it; but it was not the idea of the historical Mary which led to this pairing, but above all the knowledge that the two symbols, stag and Virgin, complement one another. The Virgin is the pure, celestial, primordial image of the world, she is the Idea. According to the testimony of his disciple Abraham von Frankenberg, Jakob Böhme, who had received the inner knowledge of sacred languages during his great heavenly visions, said that for him the Greek word ιδέα (idea) was an especially beautiful, heavenly, pure virgin and a spiritually and corporeally exalted goddess.

Virginity in the elevated sense of the divine Mother signifies remaining untouched by the profane possibilities of the existential dream, and chaste with respect to all errors here below. The virgin is *freedom from* the sin of existence, the stag is *liberation from* this sin; the virgin's way is purity, the stag's way is sacrifice.

In antiquity, spiritual virginity was figured in the goddess Artemis (Diana); significantly, the stag was sacred to her, and sometimes she herself is portrayed with antlers. The medieval Christian language of symbols needed no buttressing by the antique model; rather, both forms of symbolism arise from the nature of things.

A corroboration is that in the temporally and spatially distant Native American tradition—as Black Elk recounts in his profound book *The Sacred Pipe*—a holy Virgin appeared and brought the Indians the calumet. And like the antler-crowned Artemis, the Indian Virgin was finally transformed into a horned animal, first a reddish-brown buffalo, then a white one, and finally a black one. An Indian who approaches the Virgin with impure thoughts is reduced to a skeleton and devoured by snakes; this is reminiscent of Aktaeon, who eavesdrops upon Artemis and is turned into a deer, but before he grows into this powerful symbol, his own hounds, i.e., his passions, tear him apart. The snakes, too, signify passions, as Black Elk expressly states.

7

Beauty and Meaning

To see an animal's beauty means fundamentally to behold its essence or archetype; we speak of "beholding," since an animal's archetype transcends the realm of what can be grasped by the thinking mind. An archetype may well meet us outwardly with this or that number of clearly describable characteristics, however this phenomenon[2] is so to speak only the alphabetical letter; the meaning belonging to this letter emerges when we contemplate the animal within ourselves; it is as if we were to hear a word and distinguish its individual sounds, until finally the corresponding meaning occurs to our memory.

From the worldly point of view we can for example admire the beauty and breed of a horse, but symbolically the horse is the expression of the "shock" that awakens from the earthly dream, of the divine Instant (*Nu*) as a flash of recognition; it is not for nothing that the original meaning of the German

2 In German, *Erscheinung.* The middle syllable, *Schein,* means "semblance," as the author points out by writing *Er-schein-ung.* —Translator

schrecken (to take fright) is "to spring up."[3] The jumping power of the horse, its habit of rearing when it is afraid, the far-carrying alarm call of its neighing, the streaming of its mane (which not for nothing resembles human hair) and its tail when it gallops, its skittishness at the slightest stimulus, the fire in its eyes—all these traits elevate it to a sign of "shock" or "flashing" (to use Jakob Böhme's expression).

During his great spiritual vision, Black Elk ascended upon a cloud into a heaven full of grazing horses; one horse instructed him as to his future task. One thinks involuntarily of the passage in Revelations:

> And I saw heaven opened; and behold, a white horse; and he that sat upon it was called Faithful and True, and in righteousness he doth judge and make war. . . . And the armies which were in heaven followed him upon white horses, clothed in fine linen, white and clean. (19:11, 14)

We find talking horses in chivalric poetry also; the knight himself is fundamentally none other than

3 A meaning still extant in the German word *Heuschrecke* (grasshopper). —Translator

a spiritual seeker, who rides into Heaven upon the flash of the Now, the Instant, the sudden wakefulness akin to shock, or is cast down if he is lacking in self-mastery and bravery. A name such as High Horse, given by the Native Americans, strikingly characterizes a man's "spiritual presence" (a term which embraces both the next world and the Now).

One can compare the heart of the spiritual seeker with the city of Troy, and the celestial "shock" that abruptly destroys it, with the wooden horse, consecrated to Athena, which the inhabitants pull through the flattened walls upon the goddess's command. (Since an opportunity presents itself, let us point out that—viewed spiritually—the destruction of Troy was caused, not by human cunning, but by decree of the gods; it was a sacrifice out of which the foundation of holy Rome, the subsequent center of the Christian world, arose; one thinks also in this connection of the role played by Virgil, on one hand as singer of the heritage of Troy and of the founder of Rome, Aeneas, and on the other, as Dante's guide through the underworld. In *Troilus and Cressida* Shakespeare portrays the Trojans as noble, pious, and faithful to tradition, and the Greeks as devious, profane, and insolent, with the exception of the wise Odysseus, who indeed devised that stratagem, which, seen inwardly, was a divine inspiration.) In any case, the destruction of Troy is a great symbol of spiritual becoming.

8

Animal and Tradition

There is an affinity between certain traditions and certain animals, in which the geographical distribution of the animal species is not the only decisive factor; though of course only those peoples in whose surroundings it is found, can venerate the tiger, for example.

The Muslims treat the spider with reverential considerateness; after all, it saved the Prophet's life by weaving a web over the entrance of the cave in which he was hiding from his enemies. But even a fleeting comparison between the spider's web and the geometrical lattice on Arab copper trays or mosque walls shows that apart from that extrinsic historical occasion, there must be an intrinsic connection between the spider and Islam.

Just as the world is an impermanent fabric produced out of the unique reality of Allah, so, too, the fragile spider's web consists solely of the spider's own material; seen thus, the spider and its web are a metaphor for the highest Islamic testament of faith: no divinity apart from God. The pattern of the spider's web and that of the arabesques resemble each other in that their point of departure is a single basic form with a wealth of variations; the spokes of the spider's web radiate from one unique point and are interlaced at smaller and larger intervals with circles; like the warp and weft of the loom, the threads running from the center and those intersecting them and forming concentric circles, symbolize the interpenetration of God and the world. Similar images with the same meaning occur constantly in Arab art.

When Muhammad's pursuers took the web as proof that no one could have recently entered the cave, they fell victim, fundamentally, to man's primordial illusion: just as man takes the fragile veil of the world to be eternal, so, too, they could not comprehend how rapidly the spider had worked. But the Prophet was hidden behind the world fabric in the divine Reality, in the protective cave. In Hindu terms, the goddess Maya spread out her veil, with the whole multiplicity of the worlds and beings, before Muhammad, to divert his enemies from him. This manner of dazzling opponents occurs repeatedly in the life history of Muhammad and the history of Islam; it is characteristic for a certain aspect of the Islamic *barakah* (blessing).

As a further example of the special relationship between a particular animal and a particular tradition one could mention the role played by the dove in Christianity. Were one to unite in one creature the principle of proximity to God and that of spiritual sacrifice, thus "eagle-hood" and "lamb-hood," the dove would be produced; it is the lamb among birds, and thus associated with the Son of God and the Paschal Lamb. "And . . . he saw the heavens opened, and the Spirit like a dove descending upon him: And there came a voice from heaven saying, Thou art my beloved Son, in whom I am well pleased" (Mark 1:10-11).

What is more, the flying dove with its outspread wings resembles a cross, and its unfolded tail feathers a radiating halo, while its white color symbolizes paradisal innocence. Its monotonous call is, like the eagle's cry, more central than the songbirds' voices, and its *uh* sound expresses something alien, other-worldly, indicating the realm of death, like the voice of the owl and other nocturnal birds, or the cuckoo. From the doves in Noah's Ark to the carrier pigeons, it was moreover always a messenger bird—related in this role to its antithesis, the crow—and this also explains its connection with the glad "message" of salvation.

In the legends about St. Francis of Assisi it is said of Brother Masseo, who had found true humility,

"Often, when he prayed, he could no longer contain himself, and [his prayer] came forth in muted tones like the gurgling of a cock-pigeon: *Uh, uh, uh!*"

9

The Word of God in Creation

The custom of making a wish at the moment a ladybird flies from our body or our clothes indicates the recognition that the creatures that cross our path are messages from the next world. This custom may date from the earliest dawn of our age. He who banishes the hope of fulfillment of such a wish to the realm of superstition forgets that, like prayer, such an action requires a corresponding inner attitude. And that it also needs a special "ear" to recognize Heaven's answer as such.

The German term for the ladybird or lady-beetle, *Marienkäfer* (Mary beetle), corresponds to the central meaning of this creature; as do other German names for it such as *Sonnenkälbchen*, (little solar calf), *Herrgottschäfchen* (the Lord's little lamb), *Herrgottpferdchen* (the Lord's little horse). In its form the ladybird resembles a sphere, and the circular spots on its wings also remind one of spheres, so that the ladybird is a good symbol of the earlier-mentioned relationship between the world dream and individual dreams that, sphere-like, turn around themselves, though having only one common center, just as the ladybird's spots and its spherical form have only one bearer.

Man's environment, with animals, plants, and minerals, contains, as its most valuable and sweetest gift, the signpost to Paradise, to the life of the blessed. That is the kernel of the world-fruit. However, the man lost in the exterior world still tastes of the plentiful but perishable flesh of this fruit; for example, he clothes himself in an animal's fur, without marveling at what a mysterious and precious gift has been given him, whether by the sheep or the camel. He drinks milk and eats various delicious fruits, but these paradisally sweet enjoyments do not prompt him to reflect upon their Giver and upon the inner mysteries that make themselves known quietly and alluringly in outward pleasures. The Latin word for wisdom (*sapientia*) comes from *sapere* (taste), yet who but a few are reminded[4] by the taste of an apple or a pear of the lost kingdom of Heaven that lies within ourselves?

4 In German *erinnern*, literally, "lead inwards," as the author points out in the original text. —Translator

The fiftieth rune of the Finnish *Kalevala* relates that after tasting a bilberry, the beautiful, saintly, pure virgin Marjatta conceives and gives birth to a king; in this transformation of the story of Mary a great mystery is touched upon: the earthly berry or fruit as the Word of God.

Fourth Meditation

�֎ ✖ ✖

The Soul on
Its Peregrinations

1

Of the Poor Souls

The individual, visible eagle is only a tiny and fleeting glimpse of "eagle-hood." The very fact that new eagles are constantly coming into being shows how little the individual bird can exhaust the divine Idea "eagle"; but in addition, within "eagle-hood," the entire eagle species is no more than a grain of sand in the desert. And the same could be said of every living being: it glimmers like a tiny spark on the outermost edge of a divine Idea, and is extinguished again in a flash. That is true also of man as an individual: within Universal Man or the archetype "Man," he is no more than a drop in the world ocean.

One speaks rightly of a "poor" soul, and rightly of the infinite, merciful Goodness of God, who gives each soul what it needs. The soul of a fly can do nothing with the body of a human; but it possesses wisdom enough to master its *fly* body.

Exactly as a thirsty man drinks water, without knowing water in its ultimate mystery or being able to create it himself, so, too, the poor soul drinks its body, without understanding its ultimate secret or being able to create it.

But the thirst quenched by the soul is the yearning for a particular glimpse, a particular aspect of God; and God in His infinite goodness stills this thirst. Is there a more powerful expression of divine Mercy than the allotment to the diverse souls of precisely those bodies to which their wisdom is adapted? That nothing else is expected of the worm's soul than the worm's existence? That an eagle's existence is granted to a soul striving for nearness to God, yet able to bear it only when protected by "forty thousand veils"?

The souls drink the possibility of their earthly body; God gives himself to them completely, yet veiled, according to their capacity of comprehension, as one administers medicine to an invalid with consideration for his condition. Yes, God leaves part of his creatures' thirst intentionally unquenched, in order to show them that in truth they do not yearn for this or that of His outward manifestations, but ultimately for Himself.

The unsatisfied yearning drives souls forwards; for its sake they keep the body in constant unrest and finally flee it, in order to seek further outside it.

2

Levels of the Yearning for God

Within the earthly world we see levels of mobility, with the higher beings seized more strongly than the lower beings by yearning for God, in all its often strange guises. The mobility of animals, for example, shows a higher rank in their souls vis-à-vis those of plants which are bound to one spot, and again, the growth of plants manifests a greater degree of yearning for God than the generally passive transformation of minerals.

The movement of the stars is also passive, nonetheless, the power of attraction which governs them is also a form of yearning for God that vibrates through the entire universe. Dante's phrase *"l'amor che muove il sole e l'altre stelle"* (the Love that moves the sun and the other stars) does not stem from simple theological reflection, according to which the ground of the whole world, and thus also that of the stars, is divine Love; no, this interpretation of the movement of the stars is spoken from the direct contemplation of a visionary—were the stars immobile, they would be gods, since they are not gods, they seek the Divine outside themselves, they move, driven by the yearning for God and his infinite Love. Everything that has emerged from God streams back towards

Him and is thus mobile. The stars' repetition of their eternally identical orbits is like the attempt to remain mindful of the Center from which all has arisen; we find the counterpart to this in the religions of man, in the sacred custom of circumambulation of a center, e.g., that of the Muslims around the Kaaba, or the Native American Sun Dance.

3

Of the Paradise of the Animals, Plants, and Minerals

By virtue of the yearning for God that dwells in them, a saint such as Francis of Assisi felt himself to be brother of all creatures, of water, fire, the stars, and the animals. If by speaking to a dangerous wolf he was able to render it peaceable, this was because God spoke to the wild beast through the saint; God's voice made the wolf realize that its rapacity had been at bottom nothing but a form of yearning for God, and now it, too, felt itself to be the brother of the saint and his disciples, and ceased its killing.

We may point out here the taming effect of the word in dealings with many animals. Adam's naming of the beings and things in Paradise was an initiation that connected these creatures with the spiritual center of the earthly world and opened the way to the kingdom of Heaven for them. The fall of man from Paradise was a fate of colossal dimensions, not only for him, but also for all creatures of this world, and the continuing profaning of man in the present time increasingly deprives our fellow creatures, too, of a great part of the divine blessing.

Inversely, the prayers of spiritual seekers help the animals, too; the many conversions of animals of which the life histories of saints tell us, are testimonies thereto. All these animals—the lion of St. Hieronymus, the fish to which St. Anthony preached, the wolf of St. Francis, and many others—became beatified through the connection with the divine Center, like their ancestors in Adam's paradise. The same holds for the many withered plants mentioned in legends, which suddenly began to flourish again under the influence of the divine blessing.

It is even told of rocks which sustained the footprints of prophets or saints, that they, too, received grace. This applies to the rocks in the legend of the venerable Bede. When Bede was almost blind, a youth led him into a valley full of rocks and said to him mockingly that a great crowd of people was waiting for his sermon. The venerable man began at once to preach fervently, and when he had finished, the rocks called out in place of the non-existent people, "Thou hast spoken well, venerable father." Some interpreters believed they needed to explain that it was angels who gave this reply, not rocks. They forgot the saying of Christ: "I tell you that if these [i.e., the disciples] should hold their peace, the stones would immediately cry out" (Luke 19:40).

During the Night Journey to Jerusalem, Muhammad prayed upon the cliff al-Saffara, into which his foot was imprinted. The footprint was later fitted with a cover of gilded wire.

One can for example imagine the paradise of the rocks and that of the plants thus: that they see their own beauty in the next world and can eternally enjoy therein an elevated glimpse of God, whereas on earth, since they have no eyes, their own beauty of form and color remains invisible to them.

One can for example imagine an animal's paradise thus: that the animal possesses human language (the sacred primordial language) and has in greater or lesser plenitude realized the archetype of which it was the earthly expression, e.g., St. Hieronymus' lion, "lion-hood"; for this reason also, the impermanence suffered by the individual animal falls away, insofar as the essence is eternal and inexhaustible; the lion would eternally be God's herald and His emblematic animal amidst the blessed.

On the other hand, there are animals, plants, and minerals that are accursed; it is only that contemporary man is usually too obtuse to sense the rank, subtle vapor exhaled by certain ill-reputed places, animals, plants, and minerals.

When Nietzsche reproached Christ for injustice because he cursed an "innocent" fig tree merely because it had no fruit ready when the Son of God was parched with thirst, he forgot that another fig tree, however withered it may have been beforehand, would have borne fruit under the hands of the Redeemer. But this one fig tree closed itself to the miracle, although it was the only one among hundreds of thousands that God encountered. Thus it became a symbol of the soul that closes itself to God.

4

Centrality

The expression of the center in a creature's form and nature raises it high above less central or anti-central beings, even when the latter belong to a higher order of life. Thus there are types of minerals that are superior to certain plants by virtue of their composition alone; is it not better to be a gemstone than for example a flesh-devouring plant with its perfidious traps and viscous surfaces, or a poisonous plant such as the deadly nightshade?

Better to be a rose, whose luminous color and fragrance are presentiments of Paradise, not compromised even by its thorns, than a mosquito, which, contrary to the rose, can walk and fly, but despite the miraculous construction of its wings, antennae, etc., incarnates a relatively one-sided, peripheral possibility.

And finally, it is surely preferable to be a good cat than a bad human being, e.g., a Judas Iscariot; but one need not go to such an extreme, the masses of men fallen away from God would be glad on the Day of Judgment if they could escape into the lighter responsibility of an animal. From the point of view of the man who does not care about the journeying of an animal's soul, the animals appear to crumble into dust. And therefore, according to the Koran, the unbeliever wishes on the Day of Judgment: "On that day the man glimpses what his hand has sent ahead of him, and the unbeliever says, Oh, if only I were dust!" (Koran 78:41). And in Marlowe's tragedy, *Faust*, the protagonist expresses himself very similarly before the devil casts him into hell:

O soul, be changed into little water-drops,
And fall into the ocean, ne'er be found!

5

Of the Soul's Journeying

By virtue of their heavenly essence, the other living beings are signs for man of the divine Qualities, or—on another plane—the joys of Paradise. For example crystal "re-minds" us[1] of the divine Quality in virtue of which Pythagoras called God the Geometer, namely, the wisdom of the Master Builder of the world. At the same time, on the level of Paradise, the crystal makes us think of the "heavenly Jerusalem," the city in which the multiple is brought together into a unity according to a sacred plan, causing the splintered fragments that succeed each other in duration to come together as a whole in simultaneity. In the heavenly Jerusalem the beatified soul beholds the perfection of the divine Creation; the city is full of jewels, beings, and things that have crystallized out of opposing tendencies, and have found their *raison d'être*.

The rose, like wine or fire, indicates secret Knowledge, surpassing all human understanding, and intoxicating like the scent of roses. On the level of Paradise, the rose recalls the image of the Garden

1 See Third Meditation, section 3, note 1, p. 55. —Translator

of Eden. If the heavenly Jerusalem represents the perfection of the divine Creation, the Garden of Eden is an expression of the divine Primordiality; there the saved soul sees all beings and things in their celestial roots, thus in the innocence, freshness, and youthful beauty in which they were created in the beginning. The garden is full of fruits: they are the knowledge that fall to man in the proximity of God.

The God-intoxicated Persian poet Omar Khayyam said:

Only the drunk hear what the rose says—
A fool, a narrow heart does not perceive it.
Betray not the rare secret,
In drunkenness we contemplate the brightest
Light.

In sacred images the divine Mother is often surrounded by roses; if she is seen as the manifestation of divine Innocence (in the sense of freedom from all existential errors) then the roses signify the divine Knowledge that blooms in the proximity of this heavenly freedom from error, and that forms a circle, i.e., an eternal, indestructible form that cannot be lost, or, in other words, is "real" (not merely symbolical and impermanent like human thoughts, for example).

When the rosary is prayed, the celestial roses of Knowledge glide—at first sight—with the rosary beads and the corresponding formulas through the believer's hand, or, interpreted further, through the spiritual instrument of his understanding, his notion of the next world; however, seen from within, the core of man's soul is the cord over which, in eternal Compassion, the hand of the divine Mother allows the roses of paradisal Knowledge to glide.

If one seeks an earthly image for the divine Mother's particular kind of supernatural compassion, one could perhaps cite the experience of a man who is excluded from society because of his crimes, and when he encounters an innocent child who is situated beyond good and evil, bursts into tears and remembers his own childhood; similarly, when a man ensnared in existence thinks of the divine Mother, he remembers his own paradisal origin.

Let us take the lion as a third example: it is the letter representing the divine Glory; in Paradise its voice is the trumpet of resurrection, and the gold of its fur and its broad countenance are so to speak the color and the gaze of Eternity.

On the other hand, if we consider mineral, plant, and animal as *individuals*, as poor souls banished into a particular body, they show us, in endless variations, the tragedy of hopeless wandering in the labyrinth of the world; insatiable longing drives them from disappointment to disappointment, without curing them of the basic illusion: belief in an existence outside God. When they die, they may well have exhausted certain earthly possibilities—the outward sign of a certain agreement with death is that if possible they withdraw in their last hours into solitude and concealment; in this they are more pious than the man who has fallen away from God and, full of ultimate despair, recoils from death—but their souls merely flee into other existential possibilities instead of higher realms. If their suffering in life was very great (if they had to bear torture by human beings, for example) they may seek a freer situation than that from which they escaped. But often, especially in the case of very low beings, habit induces them to continue living out the same limitation in virtually endless succession—not on earth, but in other states corresponding to them. (The doctrine of the transmigration of souls by no means presupposes a return to this earth, rather it can be linked to entirely different worlds imperceptible to the five senses; the designation of posthumous lives by animal names would then have only a symbolical meaning.)

It is a unique, indeed an improbably great, favor for a soul to be born into a central existence as a human being. But on the other hand, the loss signified by bypassing the true human vocation is also incalculable. The human soul that does not enter the paradisal or divine Center through the narrow gate is hurled back into the dark peripheries of existence, if it does not fall into the very night of damnation.

Within the Hindu tradition the law of Manu predicts—according to a man's spiritual disposition and attitude—on which level he will reappear after death; for an apparently slight fault, the penalty can mean thousands of years of wandering in insect-like states, for example. To grasp the justification for this severity, one must take into account that it is not the act itself that is the cause of this long chain of rebirths, but the tendency to perversion manifested in the sin committed, which can continue to have an effect in the soul even posthumously, so that the soul is so to speak magnetically attracted and ensnared in a correspondingly "alienated" world. If the sinner is able to purify his soul during his lifetime through sacred knowledge or through sacrificing his inferior instincts, the gates to higher and more luminous kingdoms open to his soul after death.

And apart from that, even if the banishment of the human soul into animal bodies can extend over unimaginably long periods of time, this interval is nonetheless limited in most cases, according to the law of Manu, and ultimately ends with a return to a central human-like state; in this interval are manifested the blessing and protection that the Hindu tradition affords its adherents even after death: the journey through alien existential forms becomes an expiation similar to that of purgatory. In any case the fate of a lower rebirth is still incomparably milder than that of damnation, which has its place in Manu's law also.

The protection of the former human soul on its peregrination through distant states is closely connected in the Hindu tradition with a general care of animals; were one to coerce a Hindu (to which there is a tendency today!) into deviating from his vegetarian diet and slaughtering animals on profane grounds, e.g., during famines, the consequence would doubtless be that the wandering souls would be cut off from their tradition and thereby from expiating and purifying means, thus bringing them, in the true sense, into a situation in which they could not be saved, similar to that of Catholic souls in purgatory, if the church chose to desist from prayers and masses in their favor.

The conceit with which, in the name of humanism,[2] many people today accept their

2 In German, *Menschenvergöttung*, literally "divinization of man." —Translator

humanity as their own merit and an automatic right, causes them to find the idea of the transmigration of souls odd, "disgraceful," and alienating. And indeed, if one suddenly considers reality without prejudice, so to speak from its own point of view, instead of from the hereditarily unilateral human angle, it must seem "sense-less," that is, negating sense as perceived by the habitual narrow field of vision.

He to whom the possibility of a human being becoming an animal seems an unprecedented impudence should think for a second at least of the innumerable souls all around him who, as animals, plants, or minerals, have to live out a—comparatively—poor existence: do they not have the right to protest also?

How much more sense of reality is shown by the all-encompassing compassion of Buddha's disciples, as opposed to the infatuation of modern "humanists" with themselves, exalting man like an island out of a sea of indifference!

The flight of certain souls after death into animal bodies results logically from the tendencies dominating them, just as the fall into damnation results logically from the self-divinization of man.

6

Of the Grace of Extinction

The fact that rebirth as an animal or plant is—from the human viewpoint—a dreadful fall, does not—from the animal or plant's viewpoint—prevent the provision of a body and a fixed place within the universe from being an immense gift; God gives even to animal and plant souls a hundred thousand times more than they can ever know.

In principle God gives every living being no less than Himself (His generosity cannot but be absolute), and this is why His qualities are reflected in the bodies He creates. But He gives himself cautiously, wrapped in forty thousand veils, so as not to drive weak, small souls to madness by glimpsing Him.

The soul of the spiritual seeker is without doubt greater than that of some animal or other, yet madness also threatens it, if it were suddenly to see God in his Reality. It is not for nothing that Moses covered his head before speaking with God.

Just as God gives himself totally to the soul that, without being aware of it, seeks Him within becoming, within the many-colored veil of Maya, so, too, He gives Himself totally to the soul that seeks Him in extinction, in the unveiling of His countenance and consciously; but just as He conceals Himself carefully from the unconscious seeker behind the symbols of Creation and simultaneously reveals Himself in them, so, too, he conceals himself from the consciously seeking soul behind the divine Word of the sacred traditions and simultaneously reveals Himself in It.

7

Circle and Inward Spiral

Movement within Creation, from the path of the stars to the combat of rutting stags, from the cycle of water to the journeys of migrating birds, from the licking of flames to the lion's hunting—all this becomes a freely spiraling sacred dance, since this movement, unconsciously and only remotely perceived, revolves around God as its sovereign Center.

In fog, or when blindfolded, man turns in circles; the paths of many animals, too, lead back in a circle to the den they have left. The urge to rotate in circles relates to the slight deviations of the human or animal form from symmetry relative to the central Axis. Were there complete symmetry, man would walk straight ahead in the darkness, as would those animals; it is profoundly significant that irregularities in the structure of their bodies cause their paths to lie around a hidden Center, as if their own imperfection brought them to humility and acknowledgment of a Center lying outside themselves.

Indeed, the medieval architects avoided rigid regularity in their buildings; to express earthly humility, they deviated from this, though not arbitrarily, but following a sure inspiration, so that the formally rigorous disposition was so to speak vitalized by a vibration permitting it to breathe.

On the other hand, within the religions, the movement of the world and of man can be recognized progressively and increasingly as a true "path-finding,"[3] as the flowing into a Path, as a spiral tending in ever-tighter circles towards the Center.

A symbol for the Way towards the saving Origin is Ariadne's thread, which guided Theseus and the youths held captive by the Minotaur out of the corridors of the labyrinth. A German tradition relates of the ninth-century Kaiser Karl III that he was led safely in a dream through the valley of hell by a white angel holding a long golden thread that glittered like a star; there he saw his ancestors expiating their sins, seated in fountains of fire. One speaks also of

3 The German word for movement, *Bewegung*, contains the word *Weg*, meaning way or Path, as the author points out by writing *Be-weg-ung*. —Translator

the "chain" (in Arabic, the *silsilah*), the initiation, which signifies the transmission of divine blessing through the sequence of the generations; this chain can, however, be understood from the viewpoint of the individual as a saving rope, mooring him in the world ocean to the rock of Eternity.

The religions add nothing to the divine Creation; rather, their secret lies simply in their establishing, in a correct and effective manner, a connection between existential movement, the dance of the Universe, with the divine Word, i.e., with the divine Center of that movement. The purpose of religious precepts is only to ensure the unaltered transmission of the divine Word by the believers, and on the other hand, to take meticulous account of the nature of the movements of the Universe. Through constant, or at least regular, concentration on the Word of God (in the invocation of the divine Name in the traditional manner, in prayer, and in recitation of sacred formulas) the universal Center begins to shine in man's heart, and by following the rituals and laws revealed by God Himself, the circular paths upon which man moves outwardly, begin, at first almost imperceptibly, but then more and more markedly, to bend inwards, towards the Center, towards the Light in the heart.

As the simplest example, we can take man's trajectory through life; from birth onwards he is in a process of aging, indeed, aiming for death, dying. As a cycle, life cannot lead beyond itself; when it is at an end, a cycle would have to be joined to it, in the sense of the transmigration of souls, though a man's inner tendency would possibly lead to a loss of the human state—a "tendency" in the sense of a descending movement, a downward course.

But if the life cycle begins to curve inwards under the influence of the divine Word, then aging and dying represent an exchange of the outward for the inward, a gradual existential sacrifice in favor of drawing nearer to the Center, to God. Life is transformed into a gliding into the paradisal, or even divine, Center.

But in addition to life, all other universal movements can be transformed into "paths": the day can change from a cycle into a spiral by observing fixed prayer times, so that its end, the hour of dusk, leads to a contact with the Center; or the year, when it is organized according to sacred history, can flow into a dominant center-point.

There is transformation in life's diverse manifestations also: whereas, for example, purely profane thinking moves in a circle, at a constant distance around the Center, traditional thinking can be compared to an inhaling and exhaling that arises from the Center and returns to It. This alternation also characterizes the sciences sanctified by tradition: in contrast to the modern, purely profane sciences, which merely gather and classify facts, they lead all phenomena back to their meaning, i.e., to God, and derive all perspectives of contemplation from Him. Or compare purely profane music with sacred music! The former is a circle, complete in itself, but the latter continually dies away in the silence of the Center; it conveys the experience of brokenness.

8

Tradition and Satan

Christ could say, "my yoke is easy, and my burden is light" because the religions use as their departure point what man must endure, come what may.

A saying of Muhammad has been handed down: "Religion is easy." And he said to his favorite wife Aishah, "Only so much is imposed upon you as you have the strength for. By Allah, Allah does not tire, but you tire; He likes best an attitude in man which he can maintain in the long term."

It is an invention of Satan that the spiritual Path is "difficult" or even "humanly impossible"; the religions have always taken account of all human types and all degrees of inner strength. The saying "under the crosier is the good life" which was applied in the Middle Ages to the clement temporal government of the bishoprics, could easily be generalized and said of life within the framework of a revealed religion. The crosier, in the literal sense of a shepherd's crook, is characterized by the spiral, the way into the Center, and it is of a piece with the all-encompassing nature of God that this spiral, this way inwards, can begin at any individual point in the universe; just as St. Francis of Assisi's bad wolf was converted, so too, the most repudiated and desperate person can find his way back to the Path; the distance from him to God is no further than from any other point in divine Creation.

However, what holds man back from the spiritual Path is the devil's whispering. Satan, an outstanding connoisseur of souls, persuades the strong and the stubborn that they have no need of the Path— they need rely only on themselves, not on religion; and he robs the weak of the last of their courage by representing the Path as so steep and stony that no reasonable man could hope to walk it without falling into the depths. He continually persuades those who are of good will but indecisive to postpone the execution of their good intentions, until finally it is too late. Those who are unhappy have their bad experiences ceaselessly held up to them by him, and he constantly entices them with new possibilities for enjoying life, so that no time remains for God. If they wish to turn to God, he produces in them a leaden fatigue (which of course soon vanishes by dint of serious concentration); if on the other hand, they aspire to worldly goals, he doubles their strength.

As the highest, though fallen, angel, Satan is very much at ease with divine things and knows how to confuse people with sanctimonious sayings. He reinforces the credulous in their superstition that God, in His mercy, will overlook everything they do; he convinces the doubters that God in his other-worldliness is so distant from them that every attempt to gain a hearing with Him is hopeless from the outset.

When one has found one's way to God within the divine Word, within a revealed religion, it is easy to see through Satan's machinations: every thought that would divert the believer from his Path is the devil's whispering, however astute and carefully-weighed the reasons may appear. Certainly, the devil's weapons are strong: he can alarm souls and, for example, storm them from all sides. He can incite a crowd of people to coerce an individual into participating in group crime, by means of threats and violence. Even more dangerous are his attacks upon the intermediate domain between body and soul, the torturous dreams and hallucinations with which he tries to undermine man's inner health.

The spiritual man's defense is based upon his not needing to acknowledge any defeat he has suffered at the devil's hands as definitive; for the way inward, to God, opens anew in each moment and at every point in the world fabric. One thinks of Christ's disciples, each of whom was a spiritual center for humanity. What a defeat it was, when they fled in horror at the seizure of their Lord and Master in the Garden of Gethsemane. "Then all the disciples forsook him, and fled." What a defeat, the three denials of Peter and the doubting of Thomas. But their greatness lay in the fidelity with which they repeatedly started anew, despite this stumbling; through this perseverance they finally attained the heavenly crown.

9

Of the Might of Religion

All circumstances of life and destiny must, in the case of a man seized by the divine Word, concur with the transformation of a closed circle that is its own prisoner, into a spiral open towards the interior. A man who has submitted in good faith to the divine Word—in whatever form among the great traditions of humanity—feels a remarkable and wonderful change occur in the conditions of his existence; seen from outside, his life may seem to be composed of coincidences, however, seen from inside, what meets him is revealed increasingly as the expression of a unified guiding—a schooling, if one will, in dis-illusionment, in awakening from the dream of world and life. Even his weaknesses become helpers, masters, teaching him self-knowledge and humility, and allowing him to recognize the One God's power all the more. And even Satan's attacks on him suddenly contain a meaning exactly opposite to that attributed to them by the evil one: they become alchemical processes from which the soul emerges refined and ennobled. Just as the devil hoped to destroy Christ through Judas's betrayal, but in truth only assisted in bringing to completion the work to which hosts of saints and believers owe their deliverance from the world's madness, so, too, he strives to make every individual believer fall, with the sole result that he ends up under the feet of his victim, like those dragons or devils on medieval sculpted pillars which serve as footstools elevating the figures of saints.

On the path inwards, nothing can befall the spiritual seeker for which he is not ready; for example, martyrdom overtakes no one without inner strengthening from God, and apart from martyrdom there are countless other gateways to beatitude, suited to the nature of the particular soul. One may say with Heinrich Suso: Christ required that "Each man bear *his* cross," he did not require that "Each bear *my* cross."

When Christ addressed his disciples with the greeting "Fear ye not," the cloud of hesitation, tepid faith, faint-heartedness, and defeat with which the devil tries to obfuscate the way to God was dispersed.

10

Of the Jewel of Misery[4]

In an age such as ours, where even the appointed guardians of tradition profoundly misunderstand it and dissociate themselves "grandiosely" from the innocence of childhood, and where large sectors of science and art have long since broken with it completely, as from a beautiful but inadequate dream, it seems the centrifugal forces far outweigh the centripetal forces; dissipation predominates, not only

---

4 The German word used here for misery is *Elend*, derived from the Old High German *elilenti*, meaning sojourn in a foreign land or exile. —Translator

in the sense of vice, which, from being considered a disease of the soul (as it was formerly, has become a consciously and coolly cultivated, and so to say scientific, experiment, or a *Weltanschauung* of supposed freedom—no, the word taken in the much more fundamental sense of a scattering, of a loss of the Center. In place of the *philosophia perennis*—the primordial doctrine that transcends every articulated definition, lying behind all the diverse traditional forms and illuminating them from within—emerges a jumble of far-fetched doctrinal opinions and assertions which for the most part no longer even venture to make a claim on truth, but pose as mere aids to thinking ("working hypotheses"), nevertheless impatiently demanding acknowledgment and emulation.

Spiritual inspiration fired by divine revelation, by God's Word, retreats from mere experience as a means to knowledge; thus, by traversing the outer circumference of the world, one experiences or gathers facts, without necessarily connecting them to the Center, relating them to a unified significance, to God; the consequence is a desert of factual knowledge over which no one any longer has an overview, let alone an interpretation.

In the face of this hubbub a young person wishing to hold conscientiously to the saying, "Test everything, and retain the good," must despair. The inner incoherence of the contents of thought and knowledge manifests outwardly in the life of society, the state, and commerce, as incurable disorder, as a succession of violations of the soul and of unwarranted expectations, the fulfillment of which costs man no less than his humanity. Only strenuous effort, with a desperate "despite it all!" will keep the general perplexity, despair, and apocalyptic mood under control.

In empty worldliness and shadowy unreality, the soul filled with longing for God feels wretched, "in a foreign land," exiled, homeless.

But with this feeling of alienation, sad as its cause may be, a precious jewel is given to the soul, a bitter but healing draught against the illusion of the here-below. Once again the devil reveals himself as the spiritual seeker's involuntary helper. What remains to the seeker but to withdraw his longing for beauty, nobility, spirit, greatness, and elevation from a world in which these values no longer have any place, and to direct them to God alone, in whom all that his heart thirsts for is found in infinitely greater plenitude than even the golden age would have offered?

When the door opens for this poor soul at the hour of death, it is possible that, remembering its lifelong aspiration, it will—*Deo volente*—extend eagle wings and soar aloft to the goal of its longing.

BIOGRAPHICAL NOTES

HANS KÜRY (1906-1987) obtained his PhD in English from Basle University in Switzerland, specializing in the works of William Shakespeare. A professional writer, editor, and translator, Küry authored six books and several articles in his native German on a range of literary, religious, and philosophical subjects. This is his first book to be translated into English.

GILLIAN HARRIS, Scottish by birth and a cellist by profession, has lived in Basle, Switzerland, since 1980. She has translated several works from the German, including Hans Küry's unpublished memoirs, *The Young Men in the Cave*, Frithjof Schuon's early letters, and his 1935 book *Urbesinnung*, which appeared in 2007 under the title *Primordial Meditation: Contemplating the Real*.

INDEX

Mark (Gospel of), 11, 73
materialism, 42
Matthew (Gospel of), 11,
    12, 54
Maya, 72, 94
meditation, *vii*, 5, 15
Medusa, 21
Minotaur, 96
Moses, 55, 63, 94
mountains, *ix*, 37, 55, 59
Muhammad (Prophet of
    Islam), 21, 44, 52, 58, 72,
    84, 99

Native American(s), 4, 57,
    59, 62, 67, 82
Nietzsche, 85
Night Journey (of
    Muhammad), 58, 84
nightingale, 59, 60
Noah's Ark, 73
nox profunda, 39, 59

Odysseus, 70
Omar Khayyam, 88
Orpheus, 20

paradisal body, 32, 43, 45
Paradise, 15, 16, 19, 22, 26,
    37, 59, 60, 75, 82, 83, 86,
    87, 89

Peter, three denials of
    (Apostle), 102
Phaeton, 44
philosophia perennis, 105
purgatory, 20, 92
Pythagoras, 87

resurrected body, 47
resurrection of the flesh, 27,
    31, 38
Revelations (Book of), 69
Rome, 70
rosary, 89
roses, 87, 88, 89

Sacred Pipe (Brown), *The*, 67
Satan, 19, 25, 35, 36, 99, 100,
    101, 103
Shakespeare, 70, 109
Shiva, 15, 41
Sodom, 20
sparrow, 59
spider, spider's web 71, 72
spiritual seeker, 45, 63, 66,
    70, 94, 103, 106
stag, 64, 65, 66, 67
Sun Dance, 82
Suso, Heinrich, 104

Tao, *vii*
Theseus, 96

Other Titles in the Perennial Philosophy Series by World Wisdom

The Betrayal of Tradition: Essays on the Spiritual Crisis of Modernity, edited by Harry Oldmeadow, 2005

Borderlands of the Spirit: Reflections on a Sacred Science of Mind,
by John Herlihy, 2005

A Buddhist Spectrum: Contributions to Buddhist-Christian Dialogue,
by Marco Pallis, 2003

A Christian Pilgrim in India: The Spiritual Journey of Swami Abhishiktananda (Henri Le Saux),
by Harry Oldmeadow, 2008

The Essential Ananda K. Coomaraswamy,
edited by Rama P. Coomaraswamy, 2004

The Essential René Guénon, edited by John Herlihy, 2009

The Essential Seyyed Hossein Nasr,
edited by William C. Chittick, 2007

The Essential Sophia,
edited by Seyyed Hossein Nasr and Katherine O'Brien, 2006

The Essential Titus Burckhardt: Reflections on Sacred Art, Faiths, and Civilizations,
edited by William Stoddart, 2003

Every Branch in Me: Essays on the Meaning of Man,
edited by Barry McDonald, 2002

Every Man An Artist:
Readings in the Traditional Philosophy of Art,
edited by Brian Keeble, 2005

Figures of Speech or Figures of Thought?
The Traditional View of Art,
by Ananda K. Coomaraswamy, 2007

A Guide to Hindu Spirituality, by Arvind Sharma, 2006

Introduction to Traditional Islam, Illustrated:
Foundations, Art, and Spirituality,
by Jean-Louis Michon, 2008

Introduction to Sufism: The Inner Path of Islam,
by Éric Geoffroy, 2010

Islam, Fundamentalism, and the Betrayal of Tradition:
Essays by Western Muslim Scholars,
edited by Joseph E.B. Lumbard, 2004, 2009

Journeys East:
20th Century Western Encounters with Eastern Religious
Traditions, by Harry Oldmeadow, 2004

Light From the East: Eastern Wisdom for the Modern West,
edited by Harry Oldmeadow, 2007

Living in Amida's Universal Vow: Essays in Shin Buddhism,
edited by Alfred Bloom, 2004

Maintaining the Sacred Center: The Bosnian City of Stolac,
by Rusmir Mahmutćehajić, 2011

The Mystery of Individuality:
Grandeur and Delusion of the Human Condition,
by Mark Perry, 2012

Of the Land and the Spirit:
The Essential Lord Northbourne on Ecology and Religion,
edited by Christopher James and Joseph A. Fitzgerald, 2008

On the Origin of Beauty:
Ecophilosophy in the Light of Traditional Wisdom,
by John Griffin, 2011

Outline of Sufism: The Essentials of Islamic Spirituality,
by William Stoddart, 2012

Paths to the Heart: Sufism and the Christian East,
edited by James S. Cutsinger, 2002

Remembering in a World of Forgetting:
Thoughts on Tradition and Postmodernism,
by William Stoddart, 2008

Returning to the Essential: Selected Writings of Jean Biès,
translated by Deborah Weiss-Dutilh, 2004

Science and the Myth of Progress, edited by Mehrdad M.
Zarandi, 2003

Seeing God Everywhere: Essays on Nature and the Sacred,
edited by Barry McDonald, 2003

Singing the Way:
Insights in Poetry and Spiritual Transformation,
by Patrick Laude, 2005

The Spiritual Legacy of the North American Indian:
Commemorative Edition, by Joseph E. Brown, 2007

Sufism: Love & Wisdom,
edited by Jean-Louis Michon and Roger Gaetani, 2006

The Timeless Relevance of Traditional Wisdom,
by M. Ali Lakhani, 2010

Touchstones of the Spirit:
Essays on Religion, Tradition & Modernity,
by Harry Oldmeadow, 2012

The Underlying Religion:
An Introduction to the Perennial Philosophy,
edited by Martin Lings and Clinton Minnaar, 2007

Unveiling the Garden of Love:
Mystical Symbolism in Layla Majnun and Gita Govinda,
by Lalita Sinha, 2008

What Does Islam Mean in Today's World:
Religion, Politics, Spirituality,
by William Stoddart, 2012

The Wisdom of Ananda Coomaraswamy:
Selected Reflections on Indian Art, Life, and Religion,
edited by S. Durai Raja Singam and Joseph A. Fitzgerald, 2011

Wisdom's Journey:
Living the Spirit of Islam in the Modern World,
by John Herlihy, 2009

Ye Shall Know the Truth:
Christianity and the Perennial Philosophy,
edited by Mateus Soares de Azevedo, 2005